WEAVING IDENTITY

WEAVING IDENTITY

Textiles, Global Modernization
and Harris Tweed

Susan M. Walcott

Gluasad Press

Susan M. Walcott
Professor Emerita, Geography
University of North Carolina at Greensboro

Gluasad Press, Oregon
smwalcot@uncg.edu

ISBN 978-0-578-47418-2 (paperback)
e-book ISBN 978-0-578-47419-9

DEDICATION

To Donald Morrison Loch Street, weaver and piper

St. Kilda Waulking Song
I would make the fair cloth for thee,
Thread as the thatch-rope stout . . .

From *Carmina Gadelica, Ortha non Gaidheal*
(1900), in Sinclair, 1996, *Hebridean Odyssey*

A. Hattersley single-wide   B. Bonas Griffith double wide

C. Cloth inspector   D. Cloth mender

CONTENTS

FIGURES

TABLES

TIMELINE

3-5,000 BCE   Standing Stones of Callanish, Picts;
        800 CE Celts; 1098 Norse control

1100s   Blackface sheep arrive; Cloth from own sheep's
        wool for home use

1266   Treaty of Perth, Hebrides to Scotland

1372   Cheviot sheep arrive

1580   Weaving economically significant in Lewis

1745   Battle of Culloden; Wearing of tartan forbidden

1780   Clearances; tax changes lead to reliance on potato crop

1786   Cartwright power loom, spinning mills in Borders Scotland

1796   James Matheson born in Sutherland, Scotland

1815   Kelp collapses; births, potato, weaving boom;

1818   Matheson in Canton, China

1832   "Twill" pattern becomes "tweed";
        Jardine, Matheson Ltd. formed

1834   British East India Co. trade monopoly ends

1839-42 First Opium War in China

1844   Matheson purchases Isle of Lewis

1846   Tweed promoted by Lady Dunmore of Harris

1846-51 Potato famine; Matheson promotes emigration

1857   Treaty of Tientsin ends Second Opium Wars

1870   1st Chinese-owned reeling factory, Shanghai

1877   Hebrides tweed fashionable in London

1881   First Isle of Lewis tweed sold

1890   First Chinese-owned textile mill

1896   Crofters' Agency

1900   Carding mill on Harris;1903 on Stornoway

1906   Oldest tweed mill on Lewis (HT Scotland); Harris Tweed
        Association founded

1910   Harris Tweed trademark: orb, Maltese cross, Harris Tweed

1920s Hattersley loom introduced

1933   Act of Parliament defines local Harris Tweed

1934	Hebrides mill spun yarn permit, production up
1949	People's Republic of China founded
1964	Lord Hunter Judgement: All Harris Tweed production must be on Outer Hebrides
1966	Record 73,586 yards of tweed produced
1980	Chinese modernization under Deng Xiaoping
1988	Double-width Bonas-Griffith loom introduced
1993	Harris Tweed Act creates Harris Tweed Authority
2002	China accelerates foreign investment with "Going Out"
2005	Harris Tweed Textile opens in Carloway; textiles largest Chinese industry
2006	Harris Tweed Scotland (former Kenneth Mackenzie Mill), Stornoway; Brian Haggas takes ownership
2008	Harris Tweed Hebrides starts up in Shawbost
2009	BBC documentary "The Croft" w/ Harris Tweed
2011	1 million meters of Harris Tweed produced
2012	Harris Tweed Textiles renamed The Carloway Mill
2013	Carloway Mill shares to Shandong Ruyi
2016	Carloway for sale; Ruyi buys European fashion firms; record tweed sales
2017	Carloway to former manager and a Scottish oil tycoon.

PROLOGUE

Setting the Scene

". . . you cannot separate Scotland from Harris Tweed or Harris Tweed from Scotland." Bahman Mostaghimi, Managing Director of Shandong Ruyi UK

"Throughout history, cloth has furthered the organization of social and political life . . . and the transformations of meaning over time." Weiner and Schneider, 1989, *Cloth and Human Experience*

Our personal place of origin story is both real and imaginary. The location of our birth, and that of our parents who played a role in shaping us, has latitude and longitude. Where we live, by both choice and happenstance, contains experiences and our memories about them. Tales inhabiting these places are spun through time, containing strands of enduring themes and knots where time focuses on particular events portrayed as significant. The colors of these woven strands shift depending on the light later weavers of impressions choose to put on them, reframing the context and highlighting various aspects to suit contemporary fashion or the eyes of particular beholders. Are we part of a group identity, or a singular triumphant individual? Are we happier with our roots, or wings, retaining or ascending from them? Like the Russian *matryoshka* dolls that contain different sizes and faces of themselves, identity moves through stages of time and scales of place creating allegiances and our own self-image. Stories also have physical manifestations, some of which we choose to surround ourselves with in what we wear and inhabit. The story of textiles, in particular Scotland's iconic tweed and China's representative silk, displays an intriguingly intertwined development of national identity and global power that crosses several times over the last two centuries.

The seven islands of the Outer Hebrides form Scotland's last inhabited outpost facing the North Atlantic, floating thirty miles northwest of the Scottish mainland. A mix of steely gray blue and aquamarine water in "The Minch" strait signals the chilly, often turbulent approach to the Isle of Lewis, the main island. The name "Hebrides" itself signifies remoteness. Sparse low-storied settlements scatter along the island's edges. Undulating marshy moors and steep rugged hills with the oldest rocks in Britain stretch across the interior, separating the southern Harris section from the main body of Lewis. Small *shieling* huts used as summer dwellings in the past by shepherds grazing their flocks stand slowly crumbling. Furrows of "lazy bed" potatoes push across fields, and brown peat blocks excavated for fuel from family moorland plots dry in carefully stacked piles. An occasional tall white energy-generating windmill punctures the skyline in a modern contrast. Ironically this bit of modernity links back to preserve a piece of the past in at least one township that uses part of their electricity profits to provide Harris Tweed looms for beginning weavers.

The key to a society's successful transition from traditional to modern lies with building on a distinguishing cultural element embodying an identity that aids integration into new circumstances. For the humble Hebrideans salvation came from this notable cloth, dyed in the colors of their landscape: blues of skies and lakes, grays of stones, browns and greens of moor and moss, reds and yellow from local flowers and lichen. Coloring the wool before mixing it with other threads according to a distinctive recipe gave rise to the expression "dyed in the wool", meaning set from the beginning. Harris Tweed's enduring image conjures up an aristocratic bespoke British hunting jacket, resonant of imperial dominance. That its major markets today come from China and Japan indicates the successful appeal of this fabled fabric, a model of globe-spanning survival that still literally hangs by a thread.

The earliest remaining written record of human settlement here comes from Pliny the Elder, a Greek historian who wrote in 55 BCE of *Hyperborea* ("Far to the North"). A first century Roman described *Haemodae* as inhabited by Picts, barbarians with "painted tattoos". The Roman historian Pliny referred to "the Gallic provinces" as "pervaded by the magical art ... [of a] tribe of wizards and physicians." Indeed, natives used the wool spun from their sheep to create a fabric capable of surviving onslaughts by Romans, Vikings, confiscatory landlords, British business barons, and the gyrations of a global economy. Arabs, carriers of the seeds of Renaissance in many areas, brought cotton cloth and silk production to Europe in the 10th century. Wool production centered in Flemish (now Belgian) and English towns as early as the 14th century, forming a major export basis for further industrialization. The 15th century witnessed the spread of both textiles from the Italian city-states to manufacturing centers in the rest of Western Europe. Industrial innovations begun in Britain in the mid-1600s subsequently travelled abroad carried by emigrants and imperialists transferring production equipment and methods to new lands under their control. This industrial modernization raised concerns for cultural preservation in traditional societies in places as large as China and as small as the islands off Scotland's Atlantic coast that were threatened by global economic and political movements.

Textiles are an important bellwether of change, commonly the first industry to trigger a society's transition to industrialization. Traditional household-based economies needed to be self-sufficient, with a certain amount of activity involving community-level cooperation to share skills and limited resources. More isolated areas retain this self-contained model the longest. The typical cottage industry division of labor started with rural women workers creating and weaving the woolen yarn into cloth. Urban factory workers then finished the process by dyeing, shrinking, packaging and sending the material to merchants for sale. The greatest flood of workers moving from rural farms to urban factories, from a commodity to a cash economy, first encountered the ordered demands of mechanized life in a textile factory.

Societies manage the crucial transition from traditional to modern by drawing on a widening geographic sphere for labor, production knowledge and market targets. Conflicts come from the introduction of new forces: military conquest, innovations and information challenging customary practices and ultimately an individual's sense of self-worth and identity. Achieving a sustainable balance adjusting these demands is a global challenge accompanying the movement of people into a mechanized modern world. The tale of Harris Tweed, a woven wool material produced only on a remote cluster of islands off the west coast of Scotland, serves as a microcosm of turbulent times. Accommodations reached over three centuries reshaped the world since the 1700s. Symbols surrounding Harris Tweed – the orb, St. George 's cross, and ancient name for Scotland - carry the past into present in Figure P.3. Modernization's mix of sustaining ingredients includes selected traditional processes preserving cultural aspects of identity with the efficient methods of industrial mass production. A successful segue from old ways to a new world needs both. The name "Harris Tweed" proclaims the importance of its place of production, but the tale of its creation and survival is as twisted and complex as the fabric's patterns and multi-hued threads.

For two centuries, the colorful contributions of several remarkable individuals critically shaped Harris Tweed's global endurance. Their dynamic stories range from the entrepreneurial Lady Dunmore and merchant-war profiteer Lord Matheson in the mid-19th century to contemporary politicians, oil barons, and models turned tweed promoters who all struggled to promote this singular cloth and its homeland's way of life. The true survivors are the solitary home weavers working in sheds close to their homes, creating a cloth protected by the first trademark granted in Britain. The orb and cross, recently recognized as its own coat of arms, draws on the family crest of Harris's Lady Dunmore who first realized its market potential, popularizing and promoting the tweed woven on her Harris estate's section of southern Lewis in 1846.

The move to standardize and preserve the cloth woven by beleaguered crofters occurred following the potato famine and the infamous Clearances, when landlords substituted sheep for human occupants of their small crofts. Many desperate inhabitants were driven overseas, or to an early grave. The owner of the Isle of Lewis during this this tumultuous confluence of events was the wealthy Scottish business tycoon James Matheson. Riches derived from the Chinese Opium War that he helped launch financed his purchase of the troubled island, part of his Parliamentary domain.

This cycle came full circle with the contemporary rise of Asian outward investment targeting iconic but declining firms in the West. By the early 21st century a globally expanding multinational from a reinvigorated China saved one of three mills still standing by purchasing a minority stock share - an ironic twist of history coming from a formerly conquered country transitioning to a capitalist rescuer. The largest market for the most successful Harris Tweed mill is another World War II survivor: a resurgent Japan whose path to modernity also lay with textile production and now popularizes the representative clothing of a past imperial power. Well known in turn for its traditional silk production, Japan preserves a long cultural heritage of seeking balance by honoring the juxtaposition of opposing elements: the yin-yang (*aratae – nigitai*) of dark, rough, black, millet, night, and east, *versus* the opposing qualities of light, smooth, white, rice, sun and west. The honoring of both in various combinations constitutes a core part of identity-affirming elements signified by rough tweed and smooth silk. Japan currently provides over 80% of the market for the largest mill on Lewis, while China is the major market for the oldest mill in the capital city of Stornoway. This book examines how such a situation came about, and how a rebalancing could occur in an unfolding future, as the smallest mill changed ownership again and based its rebirth on a lighter, softer tweed.

How did history get turned on its head, with weaving remaining in the hands of home crafters on isolated islands instead of incorporated into industrial mills as happened elsewhere? Examinations of textile transitions in the U.S. woolen industry, along with the fates of local fabrics in other Asian countries from Bhutan and Thailand to Japan, India and China, complete this book's survey of alternative paths taken by textile transition. Textile production provides a proxy for the modernization process. Wool and silk serve as sample materials representing their origin regions, intersecting profitably in the modern era of global capitalism. The clacking of wooden looms no longer resounds in village streets. But larger looms in fewer cottages coexist with long rows of spinning machines filling beams of bobbins in modern local mills to send the weavers, along with punched patterns generated by computers.

While textile mechanization serves as the story's parallel warp, the weft thread cutting across storylines is connected to James Matheson (1796-1878), the aristocratic mainland Scot who co-headed the powerful Jardine, Matheson opium trading firm. One of several British companies that extended the country's political-economic reach in the Far East, Jardine Matheson forced open and profited mightily from China's military weakness revealed in the Opium Wars of the mid-19th century. Matheson used his war profits to purchase the Isle of Lewis and erect a landmark dwelling. Still known as Lews Castle, this structure currently houses the new Museum of the Western Isles and an extensive archive collection. His island's Harris Tweed eventually became world famous, but in the 21st century the smallest mill lay economically vulnerable to purchase by a resurgent pan-Asian Chinese company: an illustrative irony in the world of global capitalism. The 19th century witnessed Western countries interjecting their presence in the East with military power the leading edge, and economic interaction the justification. Asian economic powers 150 years later are expanding their reach around the globe, passing their former colonizers in national wealth and corporate acquisitions.

Fabric forms a distinguishing symbol of the civilization in which we wrap our belongings and ourselves: a marker of identity. More than thread is woven into the material. Clothing can indicate the wearer's circumstances, including country, income, group identification and values. Territory physically places and creates value for a firm and its product. A successful recent advertising campaign for Johnny Walker whiskey featured a young male perched on a pile of peat, attired in hiking boots and jeans topped

with a tailored tweed jacket. His hair ruffled by the brusque
Hebridean breeze, against an unusually clear blue sky, he faced the
weather draped in another Harris Tweed cloth and matching neck
scarf – clutching a glass of Johnny Walker whiskey that was the
main feature. Famous in the target Japanese market, the name brand
drink came in a box lined with whiskey-scented Harris Tweed
custom dyed to evoke the Scottish sky, moor and lochs (marshland
and lakes). This story reveals ways that individuals and nations
navigate the critical passage from traditional to technologically
enabled modernity. The key lies in the powerful place of provenance
- origin markers that preserve and market an associative memory of
a time and its related setting.

Figure P.1. Harris Tweed Certification Mark

The first impression on entering a tweed wool mill comes
from the pungent, earthy smell of wet wool bubbles from huge vats.
Another enormous room is dominated by the whirring and clacking
sound of colorful, fluffy blobs being blown dry, stretched, spun, and
otherwise tamed into multi-colored strands. The alarmed bleating of
shorn sheep accompanies accumulating bags of moor-muddy wool,
delivered to the mills for transformation into tweed. But not just any
densely woven, recipe-dyed tweed. The end product of this carefully
choreographed process becomes the proudly Orb-trademarked
Harris Tweed, a globally honored material with aristocratic airs and

a tumultuous two century long history of endurance by weavers turning thread to cloth on their cottage looms (Figure P.1). They are often absent from the history books that follow the product more than the producer. Critical to the process, weavers are often isolated or treated as an undistinguished group. Their work and reactions to it move history.

Although textile mills are the leading edge of Industrial Revolution, how did Harris Tweed weaving literally remain in the hands of weavers, a critical part of the production process, becoming a global symbol of the origin nation? How did this humble cloth span time and space, retaining its home-woven appeal through a history of conquest, starvation, opium-derived wealth and fashion foibles, and in the process embody its creation location? From the sheds of Lewis and Harris to the factories of Shanghai, they create and become intertwined with a specific place identity. Conflicts characterizing the last 150 years sharpen questions of what identity is, and to what extent worth fighting for. The concept of "national identity" embraces both a personal mental construct and a community in which one was born or chooses to belong (Figure P2).

Figure P.2. Hebridean sense of place landscape

Scholars group elements of a "homeland" to include an historic territory, shared myths, mass culture, legal standing, and a place-based economy. Weaving Harris Tweed closely embodies the latter element. Allegiance to a national entity becomes particularly important when the group in question feels subordinated or subsumed into a dominant and different group. Making textiles is usually the first occupation to industrialize, moving workers from home and field to factories. As such it forms the leading edge of modernization's dislocations and discontents. This book examines these effects primarily in the conservative society of Scotland's Outer Hebrides and tweed's surprising historic ties to distant China. A separate chapter considers textile's role in modernizing the East Asian development leader island Japan, the isolated Himalayan kingdom of Bhutan, and Southeast Asia's prosperous Thailand.

Language, or a dialectic characterizing a particular locale, forms one key component of national identity that is part of an "everyday nationhood" woven into the daily life of residents. Native residents of the Outer Hebrides speak Scots, a particular form of Gaelic. The term "Gaidhealtachd" refers to the part of Scotland where Gaelic is most commonly spoken: the Outer Hebrides, and the Isle of Lewis in particular. According to the 2001 Scottish census, slightly more than 1% of the 58,682 Scots speak Gaelic. In the northwestern part of the Isle of Lewis where most Harris Tweed weavers live and work, 70% to 75% of the population speaks Gaelic. On the rest of the island except the northeastern capital city of Stornoway, 60-70% speak Scots Gaelic. As Scotland's "national music" comes from bagpipes, and the national drink is whisky, the national dress is a clan kilt. Tweed weaving, says one poet and son of a weaver, "is a vital part of the heritage, history and future of the Outer Hebrides and should be celebrated as such." Although the Director of the Scottish National Portrait Gallery reportedly declared in a New York Times article that "a portrait of a nation is a subtle, shifting thing," his "three-piece tweed suit" proclaimed allegiance to a mental picture of his nation's sartorial identity, with long roots to the natty present. A tweed mill's display board proclaims identity to "Alba", Scotland's Gaelic name (Figure P.3).

Figure P.3. Contemporary tweed national identity

The story of Harris Tweed's historical evolution contains many strands. This book follows one thread in particular: textiles and their creation as a path to understanding the creation of a modern identity. Geographically the tale moves from wool-producing sheep on the Isle of Lewis, the basis of Harris Tweed, to the highly automated fabric factories and trading conglomerates of Japan, India, and China. Chapters are ordered chronologically, usually interweaving developments with major Scottish and Asian actors. The first stage following the historical setting focuses on the Opium War, introducing James Matheson who importantly bridges both the Isle of Lewis and China in the mid-19th century. Chapter Three details the critical transition from home craft to factory mechanization involving thematic example of Harris Tweed. The evolution of Pendleton, a prime American wool material, is added to China's continuing early 20th century modernization struggles.

Far from the remote island on the northwestern fringe of Great Britain, the major markets for clothing made from this sturdy, sturdy, multicolored woolen yarn lie on the other side of the globe in East Asia. Chapter Four adds four other Asian examples of the role of textile weaving in pioneering early modernization transitions, carefully combining traditional and Western elements to create a unique national identity. Japanese textiles' transition from traditional processes and designs to the adoption of Western industrial methods and fashions was part of that island nation's survival through the modern age. The historical development of other culturally important fabrics that moved from craft to commodity status included silk and cotton. Japan currently consumes almost 90% of the total Harris Tweed's production output. Early Pendleton wool factories in the U.S. illustrate a transition path from industrial England to a New World western frontier in Oregon. Women working from homes perched along Bangkok's busy *klong* canals in Thailand and in Bhutan's Himalayan highlands also experienced textile manufacturing as modernization's leading edge. These examples illustrate the both the power of place association and the importance of textile production as a transition tool from local to global goods.

Chapters 5-7 trace the waxing and waning of Harris Tweed production in Lewis from the end of World War II to the present as part of an overall economic picture of China's troubled but ultimately successful economic advancement. In this case it culminates with the purchase of a significant share in one of three remaining Harris Tweed mills. The final chapter summarizes the pattern of identity construction told in the tale of this hearty textile, with historic provenance and an enduring future as lessons continue to emerge.

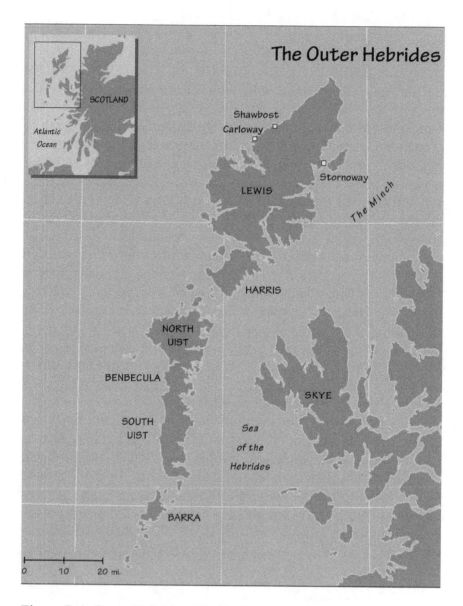

Figure P.4. Outer Hebrides, Harris Tweed mills.
Source: University of North Carolina-Greensboro cartographer

CHAPTER ONE

Spinning the Tale

"In Lewis, in particular, weaving Harris Tweed in often a major activity by weaver-crofters, whose product contributes not only a significant element of stability to the economy of the island, but also to the maintenance of the population." Francis Thompson, 1984, *Crofting Years*

Weaver Women

Mythic weavers spin stories throughout time and across cultures. Typically, the weavers' symbol was a goddess, as in ancient Egypt where Neith (or Nit) presided over weaving, wisdom, war, and "being". Men manned the looms, however. The Greek "Fates" wove destinies, but Athena reigned as the Olympian goddess of weaving. The Greek word for the vertical warp thread is masculine (stimoni); words for the horizontal thread (yfadi) are feminine, an admirable combination of the two genders. Their harmonious blending is a metaphor for marriage, and the act of peacefully creating a robe for the goddess Hera. The English language refers to relatives on the maternal side as the "distaff". For Scandinavians, "Frigg's distaff" refers to both a tool of a major goddess and the constellation of stars in Orion's belt. The fearsome warrior Valkyries wove on a carnage-draped loom. In Germanic myths Holda and Perchta/Bertha oversaw weaving and spinning, among many other responsibilities. The Celtic goddess Briganti, identified with the Roman goddess Minerva, was a weaver. In the Baltic region the sun goddess Saule spun sunbeams, represented by the amber sun stone.

Asian myths tell similar tales. In China the weaver goddess was the offspring of the Celestial Queen Mother and the Jade Emperor (parentage doesn't get much better than that). Wearing a seamless robe, she spun out the stars and the Milky Way. A notable Japanese weaver took the form of a crane, when not a young girl. She famously spun textiles for a kind elderly couple to sell. The fate of Orihime, renowned weaver daughter of the emperor, resembles the Chinese story of being on the wrong side of the Milky Way from her (literally) star-crossed lover.

Destiny and weaving designs were inextricably connected in several cultures. The Germanic giantesses "Norns" wove human destinies as well as cloth. For Hindus the goddess Maya magically spun at the Wheel of Fate. Medieval Christian Europe identified the original woman Eve with spinning. Later folktales associated weaving with storytelling and the spinning of tales. The only male saints associated with weaving are St. Maurice, an Egyptian soldier, and Onuphrius, an Egyptian desert hermit, in the traditions of Orthodox Coptics, Oriental, and Eastern churches and Roman Catholics.

Several Greek and Native American myths associate women weavers with spiders. Arachne (from whose name the taxonomical *Arachnida* classification for spiders derived) fatally challenged the goddess Athena to a weaving contest. The overly proud mortal loser was transformed into a spider. The Incan Mama Oclio was the "spider woman" who taught thread spinning. Mayan and native North American mythologies associate Spider Woman with weaving in many tales. According to a Navajo legend, Spider Man instructed them on constructing a loom while Spider Woman taught how to weave. Sky and earth formed cross poles for stringing cords. Other parts of weaving included the sun's rays for warp sticks, rock crystal and sheet lightning for the heddle, the sun's halo for the batten, and white shell formed the comb. Four spindles came from "a stick of zigzag lightning with a whorl of cannel coal, a stick of flash lightning with a whorl of turquoise, a stick of sheet lightning with a whorl of abalone, and a rain streamer for the stick of the fourth", with a white shell whorl.

In another version of the Navajo tale, Spider Woman was told that she was could weave a "map of the universe and the geometrical patterns of the spirit beings in the night sky." One day she encountered a tree sapling. She touched it with one hand which then sprouted a string from her palm and attached the string to a branch she touched with her other hand. Eventually she realized that a pattern was created by continuing to spin and wrap thread. She exercised this new talent inside her house, and was visited by the holy people to admire her work. They delegated construction of a loom and tools to her husband Spider Man. Navajo carry on this tradition of gender role separation today. Spider Woman also acquired a weaving song from the holy ones to enliven both textiles and the tools of their creation. The juniper tree furnished the loom and weaving fork. The heartbeat sound of producing the textile comes from the fork pounding and pressing threads on the weft. The frame structure of the upright Navajo loom signifies the pillars on the right and left holding the sky over the earth, a base beam at the bottom for the earth itself, and a top beam representing the associated sky, sunbeams, and rainbows of the Navajo's sacred homeland "Dineh tah."

For the Hopi and nearby Keresan-speaking tribes, Spider Woman taught survival skills such as weaving and assisted in human's emergence from the third to the current fourth world. The Keresan credited her additionally with creation of the important Corn Woman and her accompanying basket of transplantable seeds. Spider woman's domain was the underworld, split with the ruler of the sky. She assisted in creating the earth and peopled it with clay creatures including humans. Home life was delegated to women, where they spun, while men were in charge of maintaining good relations with the gods. This is one very important goddess with a critical function of cloth-making.

As the weaving deity, Spider Woman binds together all worlds and aspects of existence, creating life and sustaining it with clothing and corn. Known as "Thought Woman" in Pueblo mythology, she imagines patterns and brings beings into existence. Her stories pass on what she knows and has done, increasing in complexity and variety. The following story weaves together a tale binding a remote island on the far western edge of Europe, a country on the far western edge of the Pacific, the pursuit of opium and wealth meeting a potato famine, two peoples struggling to survive and preserve a sense of themselves and their culture. Transitioning old and new times and technology finally link the production of a proud textile with local roots and global reach.

Historical Setting

Turbulent seas surround the Isle of Lewis. With its southern section of Harris, the "Long Island" lies at the westernmost edge of Scotland's Outer Hebrides island chain. The physical geography of the Isle and its tail of smaller islands come from a fiery creation. Volcanic explosions erupted igneous material along a line of subsiding tectonic plates. Buried rock material later emerged as twisted, compressed metamorphic Lewisian gneiss. Hebridean stone's contorted internal lines demonstrate the difficulty and drama that shaped it as the most ancient exposed surfaces in Europe. Deeply etched and stressed, jagged inhospitable rocks line the uneven shoreline. Stones lie tossed on sandy beaches and narrow *machair* meadow strips along the coast. Fierce storms blowing in from the North Atlantic often disrupt sea connections to the Scottish mainland separated by "The Minch" waterway on the islands' eastern coast. This menacing passage mirrors momentous changes brought by arriving vessels throughout Hebridean history, such as the dragon-headed ones of the Viking Norse,.

The first human waves that crashed over the Outer Isles' volcanic shores left enigmatic traces. The main point of agreement on the origin of various Hebridean place names is their mixed linguistic, historic and human ancestry. Written Pict (still undecipherable), Celtic, Scandinavian, and English names show the tangled nature of this outpost on the edge of the Atlantic. The Picts – from a Roman term referring to the fierce warriors who painted or tattooed themselves – were not Celts and spoke a non-Aryan language. They probably share an affinity with either the early Finns or Iberians. A landscape of large stone structures is their most visible remains. Tourist draws include the circular pathway at Calanais and stone forts (*brochs*). Clach an Trushal outside Barvas is the tallest single standing stone in Scotland. In the first century noted Greek historian Pliny mentioned Lewis's stone complex tracing the moon cycle. Romans referred to these remote settlements as beyond their means or interests to invade.

Early Pict settlers yielded to the invading Irish Celts around 800 BCE. Fierce Vikings solidified their control of the Hebrides in 1098 CE. following years of exploratory plunder and trade. Shipments of luxury goods included the famous Lewis Chessmen. Experts assess its origin place as Iceland or Norway, destined for a wealthy foreign customer. The Uig beaches of Lewis yielded the set over 700 years after its creation. The Norse surrendered their harsh Hebridean islands to the mainland Scots under the Treaty of Perth in 1266. Clan clashes followed during an "Era of Strife". England tightened and solidified its control of these island outliers in the 1707 Treaty of Union creating Great Britain. Local clan chiefs traditionally controlled the territories. King George I put a decisive end to the periodic revolts by unhappy Scots against their English overlords at the devastating Battle of Culloden in 1745. This defeat lay to rest the claims of "Bonnie Prince Charlie", last of the French-supported Stuart dynasty. One of many measures undercutting a separate Scottish identity and tribal affiliation was forbidding the wearing of tartan kilts, handmade with cloth like tweed.

Thin moorland soils support herds of sheep, at times the bane and benefit of islanders. First introduced in the 1100s, cheviot, blackface and crossbreed sheep graze on a rocky surface that grows little else. From the mid-18th through the mid-19th century, the euphemistically termed "Clearances" involved the brutal expulsion of tenants. The land they farmed turned to economic uses their landlords deemed more profitable, such as sheep grazing. Wool shorn from these hardy Highland sheep is still used for the weaving of *Clo Mhor*, Gaelic language for the "Big Cloth" used in Harris Tweed. The distinctively intermixed colors of thread reflect the physical setting of the native Western Isles chain. The laborious process involved in its creation produces wool tightly fabricated to be largely impervious to the cold, driving rain and rigors of island life. Weaving is a solitary activity. The setting may be scenic, the yarn and evolving pattern beautiful, but the conditions and income derived are rather rigorous.

Harris Tweed's enduring appeal builds on images of the cloth and its place of creation. Roots in a particular historical provenance evoke a set of memories with which wearers seek to associate. A recent ad campaign drew on these strands with carefully composed pictures illustrating the material's humble hand-woven origins. In one poster sheep ramble wild on a grassy hillside overlooking a blue lake rimmed by ancient hills under a glowering grey sky. Another portrays a weaver working on an ancient loom inside the gray stone walls of a basket-filled hut, stacks of finished tweed nearby. Another image evokes the imagined wearer of the clothing constructed from this fabric as a person with sufficient money and taste to purchase the pricy product (typically a jacket) sported by a gentleman hunter and/or lady. Contemporary offerings satisfy modern tastes for lighter, smoother material in more varied tones, but the cloth still requires the orb stamp of authenticity attesting to their Isle of Lewis origin.

Life on the Isle was as tough as its later-famous cloth. Long left to the extortions or neglect of their local laird/lord, residents of Lewis struggled for self-sufficiency. As tenant farmers they occupied rented plots known as crofts. This system, prevalent throughout the Scottish Highlands and the Western Isles, featured contiguous rectangular 2-5 hectare strips of land. Clan or village chiefs awarded land to favored families for their use. Ownership of the leased lands passed to the State following Scotland's defeat at Culloden, and later to the owner of the Isle. Private ownership in some places recently passed to group ownership in the form of a village "corporation" in several west coast communities. Residents remain subject to a legal system that controls their use of the land and all buildings on it.

Traditionally inhabitants shared grazing ground in a township and the bordering moorland. Food came from better soil on individual plots. Small beaches of fertile *machair* land vary in size according to the ferocity of the preceding winter's waves and weather. Most croft dwellers looked to means of making a living other than by unpredictable farming. Fishermen wrested herring from the surrounding sea. Crustaceans were shunned as overly available starvation food. Sheep supplied both meat and wool. Sources of income at times included harvesting kelp for cash and/or for fertilizing fields. Cloth was woven for both home use and market sale for cash.

As a major seafaring powerhouse and colonizer, Britain long considered Lewis barely worthy of attention. The land was unsuitable for either sustainable agriculture or resource extraction. Inhabitants living on the edge of survival were often steadfast in resistance to any economic or cultural changes. It was simply safer to cling tenaciously to the known. Resistance yielded only under extreme duress. Adaptations tended to be incremental. Shifts included moving from the Presbyterian Church of Scotland to the stricter Free Church, or from a single to a double width weaving loom. Leaving the land occurred only in the face of starvation or land seizure. And then the rupture was extreme. Emigrants fled over an ocean to Australia or New Zealand, North America or the Falklands. Others sought fame or fortune in foreign wars or distant colonial firms.

Matheson's Lewis and Harris Tweed

The Victorian industrial era brought isolation-breaking intersection with a world beyond the familiar. Scots involved in colonial conquests nibbled at the venerable but ailing Chinese empire on the far edge of another great ocean. The Manchu 15th century invaders who established the ruling Qing dynasty sought to confine foreigners in enclaves of great cities such as Shanghai and Hong Kong. The ensuing wave of changes disrupted the old imperial order in both countries. The industrial revolution unleashed new ways of production and wealth accumulation. Machinery from factories to locomotion methods restructured livelihoods.

James Matheson, a gentry native of the Scottish mainland, played an outsize part in this disruption by launching and profiting from the Opium Wars. His trading company persuaded Great Britain to use military means to open a reluctant China to opium. Britain sought a trade item to balance British demand for Chinese tea. A key part of the treaties ending the Opium Wars lay in the provision that concessions China granted to any of the signatories (Britain, France, the U.S.) applied to them all. This was the infamous "Open Door" clause. China opened a door to trade leading into the interior fed by the Yangtze River, its mouth in the port of Shanghai. On the western shores of the Pacific Ocean, turbulent times and a global diaspora of emigration also plagued China. A "century of humiliation" followed conclusion of the British trade-triggered Opium War.

A founding *"taipan"* head of the Jardine Matheson firm, Matheson invested a large portion of his opium-fueled war profits in purchasing the Isle of Lewis in 1844. The firm remains one of the largest Anglo-Chinese trading houses. Parliamentary praise and a noble title rewarded his contributions to feed and export island residents during the Clearances and potato famine. The construction of Matheson's Castle and hunting lodges consumed more of his funds than did other development efforts on the islanders' behalf. Thickly forested landscaping surrounding the Castle presented a nincongruous setting on an island whose residents subsisted on heat generated by peat - the organic remains of forests removed long ago by a succession of invaders, dug out of the boggy soil with great effort then stacked to dry in carefully shingled mounds.

The movement by landlords to replace tenant farmers with sheep began in the 1780s. The "Year of the Sheep" featured forced or incentivized emigration of crofters to Canada and the Carolinas. Newcomers sought to acquire land for themselves. The concurrent mid-19th century potato famine accelerated the exodus of residents off their land and out of the country. Ministers of the Church of Scotland agreed with Matheson's assessment that "over-population" of the Isles put undue hardship on the impoverished tenant farmers. Their removal, financed in part by the laird, would relieve this burden. His agent Donald Munro earned the title of "most hated man in Hebridean history" by brutal enforcement of these policies. Raising regiments of soldiers served as a population alleviation measure begun under Lord Seaforth, former owner of the Isles. In 1793 this gentry put the entire parish of Uig (now site of the flourishing Harris Tweed mill in the town of Shawbost) on the market for a sheep farm. Not until the Crofters' Holdings Act in 1886 did tenants finally gain some increased security.

In 1832 the distinctive pattern of multi-hued twisted yarn known as the pattern "twill", or "tweel" in Scots Gaelic, became "tweed". This may have stemmed from a copy writing error, a mistaken reference to the river Tweed, or a clerk's bad handwriting. Matheson's overlordship saw the commercialization of woolen tweed made in Lewis and its southern section known as Harris. Lady Catherine Murray, Countess of Dunmore in Harris, usually receives credit for the popularization in 1846 of the colorful cloth woven for household consumption. In the first of many boom-and-bust fashion swings involving this sturdy material, Lady Dunmore successfully pitched tweed to her gentry peers in the hunting class. The material served as a suitable match for the cold, wet weather and brambles encountered when pursuing game. Lady Dunmore raised and standardized the production of her sponsored product by training weavers in a special school. Weaving soon became a welcome cash-earning substitute for the collapse of the kelp market and the rotten potato crop. From the depths of the cycle of Lewis' economy, a new and far more long-lasting economic venture arose.

Textile manufacturing serves as a suitable thread to tie together this story since it is frequently the first industry to industrialize. The traditional creation of textiles consumes a great deal of time and labor. Arduous parts of the process became prime targets for simple machines launching the Industrial Revolution. Cloth making required little capital or training and could continue regardless of the weather, the laborer's strength or time of day. The first step out of homebound self-sufficiency came with a middleman or merchant furnishing some of the raw material. They returned to pick up the finished product, and then delivered it to a customer or retail site. Lorry trucks labeled with the name of a mill were familiar sights along village lanes.

John Winchcombe organized England's first textile factory in the early 16th century. He also invented doublewide broadcloth woven on a loom that took two men to operate. Mid-16th century inventions such as the thread spinning "jenny" and a mechanical loom lifted steps of the process to a more efficient mass production level. The same century saw the first output of cloth on a commercial scale, unleashing a flood of ingenious improvements. The first weaving factory appeared in the U.S. in 1638, powered as in England by water falling from a steep height. The next century debuted the cotton gin (1793) and a wool-carding machine (1794) for untangling fleece into useable fibers. In 1813 the first vertically integrated U.S. mill assembled all production processes under one roof. The level of skill required for operating this dangerous machinery swept former farm workers and even children onto the factory floors. Workers were needed to tend the machines in a factory for part if not all of the integrated process. The knitting together of production sites in an increasingly global British empire permitted geographic competition. Wages and other place-based considerations determined where different materials were most cost-effectively produced. Reverberations looped from England around the world to China. Place competition returned in surprising ways in the 21st century as China, reinvigorated by market forces, looked for investment outlets beyond their shores.

By 1906 the oldest mill in Scotland spun yarn for tweed in Stornoway, capital city of the Isle of Lewis. Three years later the orb symbol for Harris Tweed became the first trademark granted in Britain. The original definition attached to the Orb stated simply that Harris Tweed must be hand spun, woven and dyed by workers in the Outer Hebrides. This limited production to the Isle of Lewis, North and South Uist, Benbecula and Barra. In the next decades industrialization on the British mainland, particularly in Yorkshire, increased mechanization of the textile industry. The accompanying production efficiencies posed competitive pressures threatening the Hebrides' tradition-restricted methods. In 1934 this led to a revised definition of Harris Tweed permitting only Outer Hebrides-based production. Mill-spun yarn that had leaked over to mainland Scottish firms was forbidden. Despite this economic outlet, occupants of the Isles continued to reluctantly emigrate across the Atlantic in search of a better way of life.

Global Capitalism's Bedfellows

Migrations plagued war-torn China as well. The Manchu-led Qing Dynasty collapsed with the death of the dowager empress in 1908. Warlords and a brutal civil war continued throughout the Japanese occupation of China from 1937 to the end of World War II. Awarding of Mainland China to the Nationalist Party by the Allies continued the civil war for four more bloody years. Proclamations of the People's Republic of China in October 1949 brought outward stability but internal strife. China raced to catch-up with and join the global economy, modernizing agriculture through collectivization and simultaneous industrialization. The process was not smooth. The second stage of modern China's emergence saw a more successful transition to modernity following the bloody chaos of the decade-long "Cultural Revolution". Accelerated development began with the accession of Deng Xiaoping to national leadership in 1979. China's route to becoming a prosperous global economic power came through developing low cost, decent quality and high output manufacturing. By the late 20th century China attained acclaim as the "world's factory".

Gradual emergence of the British economy from two devastating World Wars triggered market demand for its textiles (Figure 1.1). Production of tweed hit an unsurpassed high of 73,586 yards in 1966 during a boom in the popularity of British music and styles. A leap in wool and tweed production came in Lewis with introduction in 1988 of a new Hattersley loom. This device wove cloth twice the width of that produced by the previous popular model. Nevertheless, synthetic colors and more mechanized textile production sent tweed fortunes on a downward spin. Harris Tweed lost its distinctive niche in the fashion pantheon. Passed by

Parliament in 1993, the Harris Tweed Act created the current guardian Harris Tweed Authority. It further refined the fabric's production parameters as hand woven and finished in the homes of residents of the Outer Hebrides. Virgin wool used as thread must also be dyed and spun only on these designated islands.

Early 21st century reform acts such as tenancy requirements sought to encourage islanders to stay in their employment-challenged area. The hope was to legislate preservation of a waning lifestyle and Gaelic-language culture. Pressure in the previous century to assimilate and Anglicize took its toll. Average residents of the Scottish islands were older than on the mainland (21% versus 17% over 65) and less likely to speak Gaelic than in the past. The current designation of Gaelic as the principal language in 25% of Hebridean primary schools seeks to halt the linguistic decline. Although Gaelic is primarily taught in more rural school districts, English instruction remains an option in all of the Western Isles' schools. Almost half of the region's primary students are in some Gaelic medium class. As of 2014 The Isles contained 27, 250 people, with 21,031 of the total living in Lewis as of 2011. Residents ranged over 1,186 square miles of rugged, agriculturally challenged land. Deaths and out-migration continued to exceed births and immigration, with a higher percentage in the age 65 and above group than elsewhere in Scotland. On a longer time scale, the Hebridean population declined 40% over the 110 years from 1901 to 2011. Compared to the Scottish mainland, the economy of the islands is more concentrated in agriculture, forestry, fishing and construction. More Hebridean residents are self-employed. This includes a much higher proportion in 'skilled trade occupations' such as tweed weavers.

Harris Tweed sales recuperated slowly from a precipitous drop following its historic height in 1966. This decline in part reflected the fluctuating patterns of fashion. Some ill-advised business decisions also damaged the brand. In 2007 the major mill under a new Yorkshire owner limited output from the former 8,000 Harris Tweed patterns to only four. Over-production led to shipping jackets to China. Efforts to infuse new money and rescue the historic

Scottish industry resurrected several mills on Lewis in the early 21st century. The smallest of the remaining three, the former Harris Tweed Textile Manufacturing Ltd. became Carloway Mill in 2005. Funds flowed from a development agency and a joint American and Scottish ownership team. The following year the former Kenneth Mackenzie Mill in Stornoway, the largest by far on Lewis, opened as Harris Tweed Scotland. The shuttered mill in Shawbost, a bit north of Carloway, opened as Harris Tweed Hebrides a year later. A new fashion wave breathed life into the Harris Tweed industry. Unimpressive compared to the mid-sixties, the one million meters of Harris Tweed produced in 2012 signaled the fabric's reappearance on the global fashion scene. Harris Tweed's comeback combined the restless tides of trends with the technical ability to construct lighter and softer tweed fabric.

An upsurge in tweed production in 2013 caught the attention of Shandong Jining Ruyi Technology Ltd. (SJR). The Chinese conglomerate was founded in 1993 during China's tentative turn to a "market socialist" economy. At the dawn of the 21st century, China in 2002 launched a new push for successful companies to "Go Out" by investing and acquiring foreign companies. One of the objects of interest of this move, termed Chinese Outward Foreign Direct Investment (COFDI), is a focal point of this tale. In the village of Carloway, the smallest of the three remaining Harris Tweed mills benefitted. SJR's large woolen textile division noted the new popularity of tweed in upscale global markets, echoing Lady Dunmore's successful selling of the cloth to gentry a hundred years earlier. In March 2013 Ruyi entered into a joint venture with Carloway Mill.

Fabric construction continues as industrialization's edge in the current relentlessly globalizing age. Rural populations migrate into urban settings with consequences for cultural and economic change. Yet, the highest profit comes from the handmade part of the process, an archaic remnant of the cottage industry: the home-weaver. Harris Tweed remains a famous fabric trademark protected as hand-loomed on the Outer Hebrides islands off the west coast of the Industrial Revolution's British epicenter. The invisible hand of

Adam Smith, Scotland's proud theorist of capitalism, moves in mysterious ways still. The Chinese dragon liberated from a century and a half of civil convulsions, from invasions by armies and alien ideas, roams the world. Profits from recent industrial modernization are invested in companies ripe for capital infusions. And in the process generate some concern by outside observers over where this economic power may lead. The following examination of Harris Tweed considers capitalism's globalization ironies. The Isle of Lewis's mid-19th century owner used his profits made by opening China to the opium trade and invested them in purchasing this place. Chinese investment from a state-owned company with ties to India's largest (textile based) firm and a Japanese trading conglomerate saved one of three surviving mills in 2013.

The intersection of Matheson's Lewis-centered Harris tweed and China, with its own textile industry sprouts in the treaty port extraterritorial zones, came full circle. Economic slowdown two years after the initial joint venture depressed the anticipated market for luxury goods in that country, however. By late 2016 the mill's owners declared that despite a six-year surge in business orders for tweed, it was not profitable enough to keep operating. They explored if another "off-island" investor could save a fabric famously impervious to ill weather, if not the winds of economic globalization. Good news for potential purchasers came with the announcement of a surge to 1.7 million meters of textile production, from a mere 450,000 meters in 2010. An ongoing demand for high cost goods reflected the upper tier of a persistent "wealth gap" between workers and their bosses. Chinese outward foreign investments continued to provide a means of stabilizing such uncertainties. Economic conditions echoed the effects of foreign war, famine, and forced migration that hit Matheson's Lewis a century and a half previously.

Owners of Carloway Mill invested enough funds to carry their company through the orders remaining in Spring 2016. Meanwhile, the leading tweed firm in Shawbost boasts export sales to sixty countries. Ongoing attempts seek to resuscitate previously vigorous Harris Tweed markets in North America and wealthy

European countries. Carloway Mill placed its hopes for expansion
with corporate investor Shandong Ruyi's acquisition of flagging
fashion firms. For various reasons discussed later these aspirations
remained unrealized. New leadership, such as that rocketing the
fortunes of Shawbost's mill based on the Japanese market, remains
a possibility. One outstanding strength of this brand remains its
undisputed high quality. Its appealing provenance is the other leg.
The creation story provides a tale of traditions enduring and
transitioning to successful.

To Be Continued . . .

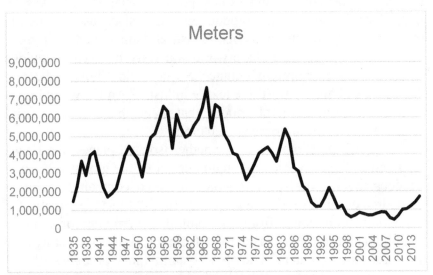

Figure 1.1 Harris Tweed production, 1935 – 2013
Source: The Harris Tweed Association Limited, Info Pack 2014

The following analysis examines global political and
economic shifts roiling fortunes in the Outer Hebrides (Figure 1.1).
An iconic textile produced on isolated islands perched on the stormy
edge of the North Atlantic characterizes this place. Chapters
examine the historic background entwining a wealthy pioneering
Scottish opium trader with his island's local fabric and a mill later
acquired by a firm with the global outreach of a resurgent China.

Insights into the underlying processes came from visits to the mills producing Harris Tweed. Interviews with administrators and workers at these facilities provided perspectives. A famous saying of the sage Confucius - "Study the past if you would define the future" – applies to these events. The quote is a favorite of the Chinese firm's president, a fellow native of Shandong province.

Questions underlying this story come from its many unlikely historical intersections. How did a cottage-woven cloth, from a remote island lying off the coast of a country that pioneered textile manufacturing and conquered Asia's self-isolated giant a century and a half previously, need rescuing by a global textile giant from that same Asian country and a small, powerful island? Japan was the first Asian country to modernize and also use a textile manufacturing transition as its industrial launch pad. All three countries were decimated by a world war sixty-five years previous to the current economic encounter. So how did China and Japan develop a globally competitive textile industry? And how did Lewis manage with a different model that kept the traditional and inefficient element of home woven cloth?

Other questions involve whether isolated places like Lewis are fated to linger outside the main current of the global economy. Or does the success of similar island tweed companies point to individual problems resistant to outside funds? Must the impetus for industrialization come from the central government of a more compliant culture? What is the role of entrepreneurs, navigating new and often stormy waters? The Shawbost mill alone produces 90% of the Harris Tweed output. What can be learned from a global network of Asian textile conglomerates in India, China and Japan? These now sustain a peripheral island's products featured in elite fashion houses from London and Paris to Tokyo. How might these lessons help other countries capitalize on their own iconic industries? Tweed shows it is possible to ride the bumpy seas of global capitalism without resorting to cheaper labor and lower quality. There is a way to avoid placing output over craftsmanship.

CHAPTER 2

China, Matheson and the Opium War

"The injuries, deceits, cruelty and evil acts of the British resident barbarians are as numerous as the hairs of the head. Now they seek to coerce the government. They have long wished to enter our city; and our governors, from their kindness and benevolence, have given in and issued a proclamation granting permission to enter. They have not considered that the British barbarians, born and raised in noxious regions beyond the bounds of civilization, have the hearts of wolves, faces of tigers and cunning of foxes, plan to take our province and only seek to enter the city to spy out the land." 1843 Chinese Poster, between 1st and 2nd Opium War

"It has pleased Providence to assign to the Chinese, - a people characterized by a marvelous degree of imbecility, avarice, conceit, and obstinacy, - the possession of a vast promotion of the most desirable parts of the earth . . . . It has been the policy of this extraordinary people to shroud themselves, and all belonging to them, in mystery impenetrable, to monopolize all the advantages of their situation." James Matheson 1838

"Enthusiastic about new ideas, a keen reader, [Matheson] founded the first English-language newssheet in China . . . Intensely proud of his Highland ancestry he spent most of his time on his Hebridean Isle of Lewis, and soon began to devote his efforts and fortune to relieving the poverty of the Highlands." Keswick, 1982

Roots of War

The ancient Greek historian Thucydides predicted that the rising power of one country's realm of influence would inevitably

lead to war with the contemporary top power. Technology and
mercantilism fueled Britain's 19th century commercial and military
expansion. Its collision with complacent China represented two
empires fulfilling the prophecy. China's hand held silk and tea;
Britain's came with cannon and opium. Excavations date production
of China's main textile silk as far back as 2,700 BCE. Reeling
machines and treadle looms were in use by 500 BCE. Silk served as
an important commodity during the lifetime of the classic sage
Confucius (475-221 BCE). Later introduction of innovations
permitted better looms, weaving styles, and more complex designs.

Figure 2.1. Re-creation of Chinese silk loom

The loom example in Figure 2.1. was reconstructed for the
admiration of tourists in a modern shop. Traditional production of
silk thread was both delicate and laborious. Submerging cocoons
spun by the silk caterpillar into boiling water dissolved the material
holding them together. This procedure, though hard on the hands,
enabled the (usually female) workers to unspool them into thin
filaments. The material produced varied by weight and intricacy

from heavy brocade to satin and damask. Adapted for a variety of uses, silk demonstrated the wealth and status of the owner.

Figure 2.2 Major Chinese waterways and cities

Early in the first century almost 300 Chinese words included the written character referring to silk. German geographer Baron Ferdinand von Richthofen in 1877 labeled a major trade route the "Silk Road". Merchants transported China's iconic product from the capital city that is now Xi'an in north-central China (Figure 2.2) to markets as far afield as Rome and India. Trade in silk and other exports peaked during the cosmopolitan Tang dynasty (618-907 CE). Silk served as the economic basis for urban and technological expansion during the succeeding Sung dynasty (1127-1279 CE).

Production continued to flourish during the following Yuan Dynasty's unification of China under Mongol rule. The silk-producing worms grow best in the mulberry and lake district of south coastal China. As part of a multi-tiered production cycle, worms munch on the leaves of mulberry trees overhanging lakes; fish consume the caterpillars' output before spinning silk cocoons. Exchanges of material commodities and ideas over the Silk Road reaffirmed China's confident self-image as a nation superior to all others that it knew about.

By the 1500s Chinese textile production went industrial, serving as an economic pillar of the country by the early 1930s. Chen Qi Yuan erected the Ji Chang Long Reeling Mill in 1870, the first textile factory in China built by a Chinese. Before then textile production was a homebound, largely female "cottage industry". Traditional self-sufficient households sold any surplus in the market. Excess production served as barter rather than scarce cash. This was particularly useful for food purchases, or as part of tax payments. Women more profitably engaged in cotton and silk spinning and weaving, as males inherited agricultural fields.

Until the mid-19th century, China's military resisted conquests that brought other countries under European control. Except for clocks, a novel navigation aid, New World products were disdained. England's Indian possession produced the narcotic opium as a possibility for balancing trade if it could be successfully introduced. China resisted, aware of the narcotic's undesirable effects. A new, more potent opium blend provided enough East Asian addicts to tip the tide of trade in Britain's favor. That the product prying open the door to Asia's greatest power lay in the draw of a narcotic was not coincidental. The lure of multiple exotic Asian products drained Europe's mercantile holdings of precious metals. Chinese silk beckoned since Roman times, Southeast Asian spices since the 1400s, the Americas' sugar, cotton and tobacco since the 1600s. China's aromatic and intoxicating tea became the new national drink of the British Isles by the mid-18th century. A London newspaper noted the popularity of the dried leaf import with the shocking observation that "even the Scotsman has given up a skalk of whiskey at breakfast in favor of tea!"

Biography of a Global Capitalist

The tale of Harris Tweed, an enduring and globally popular textile, began with the birth of a son into a prominent gentry family from the area of Ross and Sutherland in the Scottish Highlands. In 1796 James Matheson joined Europe's most militarily and economically powerful country. It was a time of transition and outsized ambition. Trade in tea and opium fueled the personal fortune of this Edinburgh University-educated son of a baronet. Opium grown in Britain's colony of India was sold to the Chinese, against their strong opposition, to offset import costs to Britain of tea. Ironically, this occurred before British growers realized that tea already grew wild in land they owned: the uplands of northeastern India's Assam province. Traders made money by their transactions, but James Matheson's novice business career began under a cloud. By 1818 Matheson was already importing opium to China in ships flying a Danish "flag of convenience".

A falling out with an uncle employed in India by the British East India Company led to Matheson's 1820 arrival in Canton to try his luck in China. A manufacturing metropolis, the city formerly called Canton is now known as "Guangzhou" conforming to the national rather than the local dialect. This large provincial capital anchored the fertile Pearl River Delta. In 1832 Matheson partnered with fellow Scot William Jardine, a former ship's surgeon. A capable businessman and persuasive negotiator, Jardine began one of the world's most profitable private trading companies. The firm still bears the name "Jardine Matheson". The company's interpreter also served as a medical missionary. The business's main import commodity apparently did not overly trouble him.

The ill-fated 1834 Napier Mission's attempt to persuade the Chinese government to take a more tolerant view of British trade in that country ended in the death from typhus of its emissary Lord Napier. He served as the first Chief Superintendent of Trade, appointed by family friend Lord Palmerston following termination of the East India Company's monopoly of trade between Britain and China. The preceding 1793 Macartney Mission to open China more extensively to trade also ended in failure. Viewing itself as self-sufficient, China only permitted foreign merchants in the Canton area to assist Britain's tightly controlled export of tea and silk.

The British East India Company, a paragon of imperialism, opened its first warehouse for trade goods in China as early as 1684. By 1730 all Chinese trade with Europe flowed through Guangzhou.

This largest city on the Pearl River delta emptied into the Pacific at the typhoon shelter bay of Hong Kong. Cantonese dialect for "fragrant harbor", Hong Kong was named for the native incense cedar growing in the area. Conflict over the opium trade with China via British India bubbled for two years. Chinese decrees forced Guangzhou's British community to relocate to the Portuguese island of Macao in 1839. Britain retaliated by taking the deep-water port of nearby Ningbo later that year. Two years afterwards, Britain successfully demanded secession of Hong Kong Island in 1841, adding the New Territories on Mainland China in a subsequent treaty designating a 99-year lease. This time limitation triggered the return by Britain of all Hong Kong-related landholdings almost a century later.

By 1836 Jardine, Matheson & Company boats carried a variety of highly profitable trade goods. Americans acting on behalf of Jardine Matheson shipped silk, rice, tea, finished textiles and cotton. The steely Matheson wrote about a captain who declined to trade in opium on a Sunday: "we fear that very godly people are not suited for the drug trade." Despite the illegality, huge profits inspired many determined businessmen to run trade ships along the south China coast. The local topography includes deep-water ports, many bays and inlets. It also provides relatively safe haven from typhoons. Following the Pearl River permits trade penetration farther into the interior. The Canton Chamber of Commerce elected the intrepid tea and opium trader Matheson as its first president. This honor recognized his leadership in publicizing their point of view to the English home country. Opium formed the leading edge of attempts to lever open the Chinese market to a range of British products. Lucrative transport opportunities beckoned for handling all goods flowing from Asian ports to China, the U.S. and Britain.

British emissary Charles Elliott initially enforced the Chinese prohibition of opium trade. British officials later treated these regulations with an averted eye. Interested parties objected to stringent trade suppression by the strict Commissioner Lin Zexu. Matheson returned to England in 1839, in part to avoid arrest in Canton for his opium trade activities. His partner William Jardine penned a persuasive plea to Lord Palmerston. Arguments for British military intervention claimed to be on behalf of all British merchants aspiring to trade with the recalcitrant Chinese. Benefits for forcing trade included reaping large rewards for the British government from taxes on imports. Satisfaction was to come from happy British customers seeking Chinese tea. An emissary sent by Jardine Matheson negotiated with the British government for a more muscular approach to "free trade". His prior work experiences included serving as an admiral in the successful 1805 Trafalgar battle against Spanish and French forces. Advocacy of military steps in the case of trade with China was less successful.

The March-May 1839 blockade of Canton forced foreign merchants to hand over an astounding amount of opium. Chinese authorities destroyed their takings during the first three weeks of June. Their aim lay in discouraging future trade in the dangerous drug. In the meantime, merchants such as Matheson relocated to ports outside China. Shipments were re-routed through more compliant Manila, capital of the Philippines. Both Chinese and British merchants proclaimed their aversion to war. But Palmerston's argument for engaging Her Majesty's military lay in compelling compensation for confiscated commodities. The sacred principle was defense of British citizens' property. Such wanton destruction, reminiscent of the earlier Boston Tea Party, horrified importers. They were in turn oblivious to its horrific effects on human consumers. Let the buyer beware. The firm of Jardine, Matheson offered their port premises in Macao as anchorage for the incoming British fleet. Their goal: to break the blockade of Canton, retaliating for Chinese destruction of opium.

Military hostilities began in mid-1839, resuming in early July 1840. Profits from opium sales went toward paying for costs incurred by Her Majesty's Navy in their efforts to promote the illegal commodity. Matheson's mercenary instincts proved unstoppable by a mere blockade. The firm continued to import opium and export tea and silk in company boats. In 1848 the shadow of the opium trade caused a Matheson nephew to leave the family firm, which abandoned dealing in the tainted product in the 1870s. Britain divested itself of trade in the commodity by 1917.

Anticipating a clash, Chinese Commissioner Lin had purchased cannons from Britain's perennial rival the French. Their firepower initially drove British forces from Canton in southern China. Undeterred, Her Majesty's navy floated north up China's coast to the port of Tientsin where they successfully threatened to bombard and invade the nearby capital city of Beijing. The Manchu Qing Dynasty's ruling empress surrendered her country's sovereignty in the face of these threats. Later ethnic Han patriotic Chinese thus claimed that China never actually surrendered to the British. Conclusion of the First Opium War (1839–1842) led to terms set out by the Treaty of Nanking. The following instability set the stage for the next conflict defining a re-balance of power.

Britain successfully waged the Second Opium War from 1856–1860. The concluding treaty fully legalized the sale of opium and expanded trade in coolies. This Anglicized term for workers carrying heavy loads came from the Chinese term describing those who "eat bitterness" or suffer hardship. The treaty opened Chinese ports to British merchants, and foreign imports were freed from internal transit duties. In the name of "free trade", this was a supposedly win-win arrangement advocated by Scottish economist Adam ('the Invisible Hand') Smith. One of Scotland's proudest native sons, Smith's statue stands along the main street in the historic section of Scotland's capital city Edinburgh. U.S. President John Quincy Adams supported Britain's "righteous cause" of opening China to global trade. Even Karl Marx proclaimed the virtue of bourgeoisie "battering down the Great Wall" to provide market exchange for manufactured goods. Was Mao aware of this statement by communism's founder?

At the end of the first Opium War, Matheson placed his China-centered ventures in the hands of relatives and business employees. His new war-enhanced wealth returned with him to Britain. In short order he secured an aristocratic spouse, a seat in Parliament for his Scottish birthplace district of Ross and Cromarty, and ownership of the Isle of Lewis. The future home of Harris

Tweed became Matheson's in 1844 for the sum of 190,000 pounds. Four years later Queen Victoria increased the popularity of owning a Scottish estate by purchasing Balmoral Castle in the Highlands. The pursuit of deer on an estate "park" encouraged accumulation of "empty" land for this gentry adventure. Resident crofters, however, already occupied the land. Uprisings by dispossessed tenants such the Isle of Lewis' Deer Park disturbance of 1887 preceded the Aignish Riot and other notable protests. Another sort of disruption came from the splitting of the Church of Scotland in 1843, ominously the year prior to Matheson's arrival. Seen as too aligned with the landlords, the established Church begat another branch in the form of the Free Church. Gaelic-speaking adherents flocked to its native language services in Lewis.

Changes in the collection of taxes frequently mark major turns in historical events. Disruptions in hard-pressed lives already lived on the edge of survival can be seen as insufferable. In the mid-1700s Lewis's Lord Seaforth declared that rents were payable only in cash. This replaced the previous mixture of cash and commodities including home spun material and agricultural products. A stunning increase of over 70% in the value of tax accompanied this blow. Crofters widely perceived the move as designed to drive them off their property. The lordly owner could then "clear" it for raising more profitable sheep, redirecting the former resident into other avenues of livelihood. "Clearances" euphemistically refers to the brutal driving out of desperate families from their homes and villages. These steps often led to destitution and mass migration to resettlement overseas, from Canada and the U.S. Carolinas to Australia and New Zealand. The entire estate of Harris turned over in 1779 to a new owner who encouraged fishing, a woolen thread spinning factory, and kelp collection. This in turn led the increasingly desperate island residents to rely on the ill-fated but vitamin-rich potato for food. Accompanied by the introduction of vaccines, the population boomed. Similarly, the introduction of peanuts to the sandy soil of China's westernmost Sichuan province, first in the 1600s and more impactful in the mid-1800s, caused soaring population growth. The demographic boom destabilized previously sparsely populated regions in both countries. Grounds for global instability took root in the soil of this turbulent century.

Bad potato harvests in 1836 and 1837 foreshadowed the terrible crop failures beginning a decade later. Poor crops continued until 1851. By 1846, two years after Matheson's arrival, an estimated three quarters of the population was on the verge of starvation. Matheson gained his Lordship title for dipping into his personal fortune to provide food during Lewis' potato famine. The main other source of sustenance was the Highland Relief Board which channeled funding from churches to more than half of Lewis' population. Authors give widely varying accounts of the total relief expenditures compared to the 60,000 pound cost for his castle residence. Estimates range from a very modest percentage of his estate funds up to a high of almost 260,000 pounds over two decades. Lews Castle's imposing structure and surrounding rare forest took the place of land formerly used as a common cow pasture. This earned early enmity for the new Lord of the Isle in the eyes of his farming subjects. Matheson ultimately funded the emigration of around 2,000 islanders to Canada through the early 1860s. His generosity came in response to what he perceived as a complication and consequence of over-population. In light of the potato famine and Clearances movement, many islanders took the escape route.

Similar to efforts later made by Lord Leverhulme, the soap magnate and next owner of Lewis, James Matheson initially attempted what he saw as improvements to the situation in this remote and largely impoverished locale. On the positive side of the balance sheet, during Matheson's relatively benevolent Lordship in Lewis (1844-78) the road mileage across the island tripled. Crofters received sixty acres of drained bog land, out of the 1,000 originally envisioned. These plots were later abandoned as too far from the sea. They were neither nourished as tidal machair meadows nor accessible for fishing boats. Matheson established several schools, but due to lack of sufficient funding they were later turned over to the Edinburgh Ladies Association to manage. He improved husbandry with imported bulls, and the fishing industry with curing stations. Changes to Stornoway harbor were made more enthusiastically than carefully, and the fishing industry continued to languish. As Lewis' capital and only Isle city, Stornoway acquired water and gas facilities, a (ultimately unsuccessful) chemical factory, an improved harbor, brickworks and ship repair facilities.

Matheson's efforts received little cooperation or credit from residents during his lifetime. Preventive measures to reduce the incidence of tuberculosis included the isolation of individuals returning from the Scottish mainland with this condition. A number of hygienic improvements related to living conditions were tied to leasing terms. These included separate quarters for humans and stock animals. Chimneys were encouraged for conducting smoke from peat fires outside rather than percolating through thatched roofs. Such measures were unpopular, in part because smoke-infused thatch was useful later for other purposes. A more basic and underlying constraint on changes came from pressure to maintain traditional ways practiced by one's peers.

Mid-point in the turbulent decade of 1841-51, the Countess of Dunmore perceived commercial possibilities for the colorful tweed made by her tenants on Harris. By 1857 she oversaw a stocking and embroidery industry on the island. Two years later a Mrs. Thomas noticed a growing interest in these homemade items. Her successful shop subsequently featured crofter creations. At the same time mainland Scotland transitioned to mechanized mill-based wool and cotton cloth production. English inventions in wool production complimented the "flying shuttles" of the lowland Scotland's Galashiels borders region.

The vagaries of fashion and history coincided to raise tweed to a renaissance in the 1840s. Sir Walter Scott's well-publicized embrace of the fabric harkened back to tartan's cultural significance. The need of hunters and their staff for sturdy outerwear culminated in Queen Victoria's beloved Prince Albert's order for his own "Balmoral" tartan design in 1853. Rather ironically the noblesse oblige angle of Harris Tweed worn by the nobility included a sense of thereby assisting the "very poor people of the outlying islands of

Scotland". Up to that point, gentry' actions had largely exacerbated rather than alleviated conditions of poverty.

The cruelty of Matheson's designated agent-enforcer, known in the parlance of the times as a Factor, greatly diminished gratitude for Laird Matheson's actions. He instead reaped anger at Donald Munro's confiscatory and self-enriching tactics. These were often imposed in the name of the Lord on whose behalf he served from 1853-1875. Fury grew at steps taken to deprive poor crofters of land during the Clearances. Steps aimed to create more grazing space for more profitable sheep led to the Bernera Riot in 1874. This uprising over the mistreatment of protesters against land confiscation became the first successful violent protest opposing the Clearances in Scotland. It also led to a judicial ruling stripping Munro of his office, and some reconciliation of the islanders with their Laird.

The 80-year-old Laird of Lews Castle left his island for the last time in mid-summer 1877. Ill health and bad press flowed from a perception of insufficient aid to his indigent crofters while he enjoyed the comforts of his new Castle. Matheson passed away on the final day of 1878. Funding attempts to assist his poverty-stricken tenants included providing them training in a variety of trades and occupations. His demise ended such subsidies, creating a need for more sustainable work such as found in the growing Harris Tweed industry. By 1881 the nearby township of Lochs registered the first purchases of tweed sold outside Harris. Small local merchant middlemen assisted in forging connections between home weavers and wider markets. This also occurred in the Japanese textile industry at about the same time. New paths from farm and field to more affluent industry jobs were emerging. Herring fishing and processing for a wider market also became profitable with support provided by Matheson's successor. Lord Leverhulme acquired the nickname of "Soap Man", in recognition of his previous success in that industry, which failed to catch on in Lewis.

Another historical twist came with the advent in 1884 of the Home Arts and Industries Association. This organization foreshadowed the Arts and Crafts Movement that later spread throughout Britain and the United States. Their shared impulse lay in promoting handcrafted items. The fashionable reaction protested what were considered to be the homogenizing and de-humanizing effects of industrialization. Five years later Scottish products linked into this movement with establishment of the Scottish Home Industries Association and the Highland Home Industries and Arts Association. A founder credited their emergence with "undoubtedly a growing appreciation of homemade fabrics." Promotion of Harris Tweed and protection of its integral home-woven aspect fit well into a framework exalting handcrafted items. It also provided a welcome counterpoint to the mechanization of an increasing number of production processes. At the same time, on the other side of the world China struggled to modernize through mechanization. Resistance to subordination by Western forces included embracing their tools, if not their philosophies.

Opium War Aftermath: Taipan and Taiping

By August 1842 Britain concluded the First Opium War with the Treaty of Nanking. Treaty-designated trading ports opened in five southeast coastal cities. Hong Kong became a full-fledged crown colony. The British international settlement officially opened in 1843. The French concession followed five years later. Both enclaves provided refuge for native and foreigner alike during the Taiping Rebellion to come. Foreign ideas from the YWCA to Marxism flourished under their protection early in the next century.

China's largest city at the delta mouth of its longest river, Shanghai was divided into French and British-American international extraterritorial zones along the banks of the Huangpu River. The Huangpu carried water yellow from transporting shimmering Tibetan silt run-off. The Yangtze River, now named the "Chang Jiang" or Long River in the Mandarin dialect, was navigable across the width of China. Chinese unhappiness with these developments came from confronting the unaccustomed humiliating foreign military superiority. Chinese faulted the Qing dynasty's "foreign" Manchu rulers' cupidity in the face of threatened British cannon fire. Signing the despised Treaty under military compulsion led to outbreak of the deadly Taiping Rebellion. That domestic disturbance ravaged the rural countryside from 1850-1864.

An aspiring scholar-administrator led the bloody uprising. His fever-addled depression following failure of the national exams resulted in visions of his true status as the brother of Jesus. Hong Xiuquan saw himself sitting at God's left hand, destined to bring His Kingdom on earth in China. Popular rage at both foreign aggression and duplicitous Manchu rulers fueled the Taipings. A number of cities fell to these rampaging upstarts. The Chinese section of Shanghai came under the rebels' control for a year and a half around the 1854 high water mark. By 1855 Shanghai was reestablished as a successful foreign trade site within the French and British concessions. Traders profitable shipped out high demand tea and silk to generate badly needed funds for the Qing Dynasty and taxes for the foreigners.

Guangzhou flared up again the next year. Chinese unhappiness with the foreign presence and penetration into their traditional lifeways and economy lingered. Britain's resounding military response led to the Second Opium War. Any remaining British grievances were resolved by the 1857 Treaty of Tianjin, named for the port city connected to the inland capital of Beijing. The Yuan Dynasty's high plains Mongol horsemen established their "Northern Capital" close to the Great Wall's grassland during their time in power. Tianjin became a treaty port in 1860, the year Britain obtained the mainland peninsula of Kowloon. A brief boat ride across from the island of Hong Kong, "Nine Dragons" was ceded in perpetuity. A 99-year "lease" agreement between Britain and China added the "New Territories" contiguous chunk of land. This arrangement ultimately resulted in the return of all British territory to China within a century. General "Chinese" Gordon assisted with the final expulsion of Taiping forces from Shanghai in 1863. His action laid the groundwork for that city's explosion as a modern industrial manufacturing site within the British and French-controlled extraterritorial zones. Utilizing the flood of Taiping era refugees that poured in from the destabilized countryside, factory owners found a ready new workforce.

Figure 2.3 Remodeled interior, historic outside, Shanghai 2012

Housing similar to European and American "row houses" was built in the cramped quarters adjacent to the owners "stone house" cross of Chinese and Western architecture styles. Shanghai's unique "lilong" alleys featured these worker houses. Their locations interspersed with relatively more luxurious "stone house" mansions for the better-paid. By the dawn of the 21st century some of these areas were gutted for retail catering to the new wealthy. Outsides were preserved as historic architecture. A "Lilong Museum" now displays row houses as a contrast to the better housing for contemporary laborers in the communist "workers' paradise" of the post-1949 New China. Some of the lilong shells converted to retail for modern middle class consumers. Symbols like the now-ubiquitous and readily recognizable "Starbucks" coffee house catered to aspirations for global "made it" status (Figure 2.3).

By 1870 opium accounted for two-thirds of the Sino-Indian trade imbalance. Britain earned trade surpluses from Southeast Asia as well. The resulting drain on China's economy indirectly led to domestic disturbances. Chinese emigrants scattered around the world. Remittances sent from the global diaspora back to the homeland and trade networks created by emigrants eventually served China's economic rise in the late 20th century. Britain was weakened after waging two successful but debilitating world wars. The successful imperial Britannia that "ruled the waves" in high Victorian times inspired entrepreneurial imperialists to spread out to overseas dominions. New factory workers fresh from their farms learned how to become industrial workers of the world. Another Westerner taught them to unite with a new revolutionary ideology in response.

The advent of capital-heavy imperialism combined with labor-rich China. Merchants promoted this exchange of human surplus rather than capital investment in Chinese factories. By the 1860s Chinese thread spinners protested cheap imports mass-produced from the factories of Britain. Competition also came from former or current colonies: the U.S. and India. Home spun yarn could not compete. Although the first Chinese-owned cotton textile mill went into production in 1890, it only passed a million spindles in 1915. India achieved that mark 45 years earlier in 1875, under British colonial administration. Chinese mills eventually came under foreign control and fell from the pressure of mass produced imports. China's nationalist transition period culminated in the brief "Hundred Days of Reform" in 1899. During that time small local mills arose to compete with imported thread and cloth. Chinese entrepreneurs and some government support financed start-up ventures. These proved ultimately unsuccessful.

The 1920s witnessed the final transition to mill manufactured cloth. Distinctions remained between the better quality products made by British mills and the less refined, cheaper products from the U.S. and Japan. Under its young mid-19th century modernizing Emperor Meiji, Japan out-competed Chinese textiles. Its vast Tomioka Mills played a key part in Japan's earlier transition to industrialization. This successful Asian pioneering movement is discussed at greater length in the next chapter.

Some similarities to the situation in Lewis might be marked at this point. Manufacturing quickly took place where a strong pro-growth interventionist central government existed. Examples include Meiji Japan and a century later under the communist regime in China. Japan's pre-World War I model included a coterie of clannish crony capitalists such as the Mitsui and Mitsubishi. These forward-looking families transformed medieval land-based wealth into new investments in industry. Modern China, represented by the example of textile conglomerate Shandong Ruyi in the next chapters, appears to be evolving to this mix of state owned and quasi-private corporations. In Matheson's time both India and the Isle of Lewis operated under a more colonial system. Competitive pressures came from capitalist occupiers and their military enforcers. In India this framework took the form of the British East India Company. Results resembled this chapter's discussion of China's outcome when the foreign monopolies left.

Lewis experienced less-than benign neglect by the British home government. Workers' fates rested with the will of their capitalist titan owners. These individuals proved less successful than centralized governments in transferring their capital in land and its accompanying people. Lewis remained caught with a conservative culture common to its Asian counterparts, but without a government's compulsion to invest in local industrial conversion. In this respect it resembled many contemporary countries. Their drive to modernize and lift citizen's standard of living seems to have stalled. Dangerous and explosive consequences threatened.

Chapter 3

Material and Modernization: Traditional to 20th Century

"From time immemorial the inhabitant of the West of Scotland, including the Outer Hebrides, had made cloth entirely by hand." Dr. Scott, 1914, University of Edinburgh

"It is . . . in my opinion rightly felt, by those who purchase Harris Tweed that they are assisting the inhabitants of remote islands to supplement the bare living which they are able to wrest from the soil or from the sea by engaging in their own time in weaving . . ." Lord Hunter, 1964, Hunter Commission Report

"Weaving has always gone along with crofting . . . economically and socially it was a great contributor to the vibrancy of the villages here." Catherine MacDonald, 2013, Harris Tweed Hebrides

      Longtime residents of Lewis recall the clacking sound made by the foot peddles on the old Hattersley loom. Croft sheds throughout the village echoed as residents worked on weaving tweed during any available hours. Itinerant instructors initiated young hands to perform various tasks in the production process. Dyeing or carding provided jobs in the factories, or the skilled work of home weaving. Vehicles regularly passed through village streets delivering spools of factory furnished thread. Their return trip picked up rolls of "greasy" unwashed cloth for finishing at the factory. Raising sheep supplied the basic raw wool. Small shed shielings for sheltering summer shepherds dotted the broad moor. This labor-intensive age-old picture of traditional pursuits could not last. A mechanized world rewarded minimizing time and maximizing profits.

Animals supplying fur for clothing construction reflect the geographic and historical particulars of a place. Sources of fur vary from domesticated dogs to breeds of goats, sheep, rabbits, and highland relatives of the camel. Migrating herders came with their wool-producers and the knowledge of how to transform their fur into human clothing. Highland sheep responded to the cold, rainy climate with thick coats. Soft Cheviot sheep were bred before 1372; Blackface sheep were introduced around 1762. Crossbreeds combined the best of both. Residents of the rocky Hebridean islands traditionally followed seasonal pursuits. Farming on leased small plots of "croft" land interspersed with fishing, herding, weaving and other basic sustenance or income generating ventures. Men sat at their loom for weaving between spring and harvest work cycles. Cash for their creations came either from their designs or under contract with a mill. Seasonal fishing demanded heavy efforts, as did farming in warm weather. Sheep were sometimes sheared in late spring to lighten their wool coat through the warmer summer months. After late summer sheep shearing by the men, women prepared and wove the wool in the winter. Reduced numbers of local sheep and shepherds now require reliance on wool from throughout the United Kingdom for cloth production.

Steps in the Process

Preparation of the wool traditionally starts with dipping the sheep in a trough for the initial cleansing. They are then sheared with special tools to remove their wooly outer coat. This task requires strength to manage the anxious animal and skill to avoid nicking it with shears. Wool from around the island is collected in a fleece-shed. Alternatively wool brokers bring it to the tweed producer' factory. Hot soapy water scours the wool, washing out dirt, oil and other impurities. Sorting separates cloth quality level fleece from other uses. Oil is then applied to replace the natural version stripped in cleaning.

Figure 3.1 Dyeing Vats

The next step is distinctive for Harris Tweed. Fleece is first submerged in a dyeing vat (Figure 3.1). From this process comes the phrase "dyed in the wool," meaning permanent. Traditional colors from plants in the local landscape reflect the unique setting of their geography. Crottal lichen scraped off stone creates a distinctive brown color when boiled, for example. The advent of chemical dyes and the move to mill production changed the process. Their adoption added variety to the basic shades available. Evoking colors of the local flora and fauna remains a selling point and provenance connection.

Dye-soaked wool is piped into a drying room. Occasional stirring helps hasten the process preparing for the critical mixing of colored pieces. Next steps consist of carding and twisting the wool strands into yarn threads in a roving process prior to spinning. Combining colors of dyed wool for the desired blend occurs according to a specific formula by weight and proportion. More spinning, mixing and shredding follows until the customized shade emerges. The large "blending bins" combine puffs of wool of designated colors until the desired shade is achieved.

Numerous machines invented throughout the industrial revolution sped this and the next steps short of actual weaving. Carding is a process of combing the wool with a surface embedded with sharp points. This regularizes the wool's texture by creating long, narrow continuous strands of fiber. Use of a cranked drum carder simplified home processing. Hand operated cards were standard prior to Wyatt and Paul's 1748 invention of the revolving cylinder that became a factory machine. Spinning with a type of spindle twisted together the long strings of 'tape' produced by carding. Their combined strength assisted in resisting breakage. Large rollers in the modern machinery comb the tangles until thread quality. Thread spun on the frame machine is next mounted onto large bobbins. Bundles of thread for specified warp and woof pattern are wrapped on beams. Now all is ready to transport to weavers for the step that will create the actual cloth. Offerings of food in gratitude for the task ahead formerly accompanied the delivery. At the weaving shed the supplied thread is mounted carefully on the loom as either length-wise warp or width wise horizontal woof threads. The weaver uses a custom guide to set up the woof's "neddles" and the warp's "rapier." A foot-operated shuttle creates the desired pattern.

Maintaining a rhythmic beat of the looming is a critical component during the average 13 hours taken to produce around 80 yards of material. A structure separate from but close to the main house usually serves as the weaving shed. Features of the production site include a level concrete floor. Windows and heat are optional. The web spinners weaving tweed were colloquially called "spiders" for their skill at the textile's elaborate creation.

Traditionally weavers in Harris were women. On Lewis, loom work fell to the men. If the men were filling in between seasonal fishing work rather than specializing in weaving, lower quality output could result. At present male weavers predominate throughout the Isle. Tweed work in Harris was primarily done with hand spun yarn before 1914. In Lewis the combination of handspun weft and mill-spun warp thread was common on island looms. Mills in Stornoway and a carding mill in Tarbert furnished the basic supplies that merchants sent to home weavers. Afterwards a team of women worked the woven cloth to make it tight and durable, known as the process of "waulking. Women preferred weaving to fish gutting, the other non-farm available occupation.

A group of women waulked the cloth "web" by washing, pressing, pounding and stretching the fabric. Rigorous activity at this stage, known as "fulling," made the material near-eternally impenetrable by cold or wet. The fabric was first submerged in a large tub or trough. Stretching material across the interior room beams allowed it to dry. Smoke from the peat fire heating the dwelling permeated the fabric. The softness and temperature of the water as well as the detergent used to clean the fabric all contributed to the quality of the end result. Their task was often accompanied by sharing food staples such as bread, butter, cheese and mutton. The hostess whose web was being worked on contributed other items as available. Singing traditional songs and sharing stories accompanied beating the new cloth on a flat surface. Duration of this process depended on the use the cloth would serve. A blanket could take an hour, or a night's work for a fisherman's wear that needed to be weather impervious. Waulking songs with lyrics refer to amusing, tragic or diverting life events. Songs also accompanied the laborious process in the Scandinavian countries of Norway, Sweden and Finland. Croft groups frequently relied on the inclusion of kin for the cooperative teamwork involved in village activities. Sharing grazing land, herding and crewing fishing vessels supplied group experiences. Together such small cohesive groups formed the basis for the concentrated geography of integrated hamlets. Ideally, dwellings functioned as interdependent communities. Current production processes involving machinery include a replacement for the highly social and extremely laborious waulking step. Social bonding had to take place elsewhere.

> "All the cloth that the men wore was made by the
> women – by their wives and mothers . . . You know
> when cloth is made it has to be shrunk – what they
> call waulking. Well, for ordinary blankets and the

like of that an hour or so's waulking would be sufficient, but for fishermen's blue cloth it was a whole night. They would start the waulking at perhaps . . . six in the evening and wouldn't be finished until ten at night, with songs going all the time they were shrinking it. Oh, yes, they had pride in their work . . .the praise of the neighbors, if it was forthcoming, was payment for all their labors." For *Tocher*, 10 in *Hebridean Odyssey*

This arduous task is now done at the mill. A tenter machine hooks and holds the cloth taut so it can be trimmed and blown or spun dry but retain its shape. Reverting to traditional labor-intensive methods, workers manually inspect the fabric, removing deficits by hand snipping excess tufts or darning to fill in absences. An official inspector from the Harris Tweed Authority then examines the final work prior to permitting the ironing on of the orb to certify that the material has met Harris Tweed standards. Started by concerns over standardizing fabric quality, Harris Tweed's orb became Britain's first trademark, proudly featuring the Dunmore's heraldic emblem.

Elements related to gender roles fluctuate throughout this tale. As often the case in textile production, this played out differently in various places and over time. Which gender performed which tasks in the production process reflected the strength required whether is involved sitting or mobility, and wage level. Factory as well as cottage industry tasks were highly gendered. Within the chain of tasks involved in textile production, women usually performed the initially cottage industry steps of carding, spinning and weaving. Heavier equipment in the form of single and later double width looms saw a transition to men's work in weaving. In 1895 adoption of a larger loom in Lewis increased output productivity and weight of the larger metal machines. Exceptions occurred by village, and between customary practices in Harris versus Lewis. Room for variation was provided by personal preference and the proclivity of dedicated individuals.

Gendered divisions took place as steps migrated to machine work in the mills. The arduous task of waulking the wool went from a crew of women socializing around a common home table to men presiding over heavy machined tasks. Shearing the sheep reminded largely men's work, while watching the thread spun onto bobbins and inspecting the final finishing fixes went to both. Applying the ultimate orb-stamped certification, a prestigious task, is usually men's work. Patterns in the Outer Hebrides in relation to Harris Tweed production varied from gender roles in textile production in different times and places. Nineteenth-20th century U.S. and Japanese mills differed from those in contemporary South Asia. In general, routine lower wage tasks with lower strength requirements generally devolve to women. As seen in Chinese textile factories, the same sewing machine can be in the hands of an experienced older male or young female worker. Work conditions generally reflected a fairly docile, unorganized workforce desperate enough to accept difficult labor conditions.

From Cottage to Mill Manufacturing

Documents from the Roman occupation of Britain in the second through the fifth century record the first 'mass manufacture' of wool spinning and weaving. Abundant local sheep supplied wool for garments of soldiers stationed in the chilly north. Prior to the Industrial Revolution the creation of wool textiles in the British Isles relied on small, scattered production sites. These occurred in personal residences, the picture of the classic cottage industry. Even the initial major mechanical innovations in the mid-1700s involved devices suitable for home use:

- The flying shuttle in 1733;
- Wyatt's machine spinning in 1738 and his revolving cylinder carding in 1764;
- The spinning jenny in 1766,
- Arkwright's water frame in 1769;
- Cartwright's power loom and comber frame in 1774;
- The spinning mule in 1779.

Arkwright's many ingenious time and labor saving devices during this early transition time period were designed for cotton textile production. The trend held for wool as well, and went global. The French Jacquard loom debuted in 1792-1801. Lowell's Massachusetts waterpower loom came out in 1813. Cotton served as the first mechanized material due to its more flexible fiber structure. This made it amenable to the routine rigors of machinery, compared to more complex and brittle wool, flax or jute. The first water driven factory was a silk mill that prepped yarn thread for weaving. Set up in West Riding, it was based on an Italian model and brought back to England.

By the early 1800s the basic preparatory practices for weaving, such as carding, were fully mechanized. The advent of the steam engine in 1785 required access to water and pools of labor. New jobs drew former agricultural workers to factory production sites. By 1820 mills spun yarn for all fabrics except jute, which was consequently losing popularity. Thirty years later the operations of carding (combing), fulling (washing, drying, applying friction to create a thicker, compact cloth) dyeing and finishing were consolidated in a single factory operation. Inexpensive and abundant labor for England's major mill towns in the late 19th- early 20th century flowed from farms. Jewish refugees fleeing pogroms in other parts of Europe also supplied eager workers.

Around 1829 tweed making transformed from a home-produced and consumed practical cloth into a fashionable fabric. Factories largely addressed the demand. The name "tweed" reportedly stems from a misreading of the Scottish tweel/twill weave by a clerk for London tailor James Locke. "Twill" refers to "a diagonally ribbed cloth produced by passing the weft threads over one and under two or more warp threads." This technique does not apply to all tweeds. Harris Tweed belongs to the rougher homespun class of tweeds. This distinguishes it from the finer dense Saxony and more open Cheviot categories. Since the late 1860s factories produced tweed for fashionable British sporting or lounging menswear and women's casual country fashion.

Popularity of the sturdy fabric produced in the home of

Hebridean weavers led to lesser cost, higher volume imitation in the Industrial era textiles mills of mainland Scotland and Europe. Off-island produced tweed cut into the islanders' treasured market. This led to adoption of the trademark stamp and certification process in the first decade of the 20th century to protect the tweed name from shoddier English Yorkshire mill products. These inferior goods overtook supplies between 1880-1914, giving "Scotch Tweeds" a negative connotation. The term "shoddy" applied to low quality goods or behavior in general. It originated in the admixture of virgin wool with recycled, shredded rags or waste material. Unscrupulous manufacturers used this method to stretch and cheapen textiles. Used as a noun since 1832, *shoddy* was a Yorkshire provincial word. Yorkshire businessmen became involved with Harris Tweed production in the next century. Efficiently produced tweeds gained market share due to price drops in the face of a US textile tariff in the 1890s and adverse economic conditions at the time. In this high age of imperialism, the association of tweed with outdoor sports promoted an image of the British imperialist class. Hearty, healthy tweed wearers were seen as indulging in leisure pursuits resulting in ruddy faced, robustly capable world-conquerors.

Material known specifically as "Harris Tweed" sold outside the Hebrides as early as 1881. Other islands and the Scottish mainland textile heartland of the Borders district also produced tweeds. Various Home Industries Associations, staffed by supportive gentry patrons, promoted production throughout Scotland. Their efforts expanded market demand. Stemming from steps taken in 1884 by Eglantyne Louisa Jebb, a Shropshire woman, led to the Home Arts and Industries Association. This organization supported handmade craft objects by local lower classes. Harris Tweed production by rural Hebridean weavers fit into a popular turn-of-the-century framework:

> *"The establishment, or the revival, of village industries, and the providing of the necessary instruction for the peasants, is certainly one of the most hopeful of any of the agencies at work for*

> *encompassing a renascence of handicraft. A*
> *flourishing village industry has the additional*
> *advantage of checking the constant influx of country*
> *folk to towns, as well as providing means of*
> *livelihood, under healthy conditions, to a population*
> *which, as has been fully proved, cannot be entirely*
> *supported by agricultural labor."*
> Cox, 1990, *Home Arts and Industries Association*

Set up in 1897, the Congested Districts Board (later Scotland's Agricultural Board) funneled government grants to support employment in crowded and impoverished areas. Grants related to Harris Tweed covered vats for dyeing the yarn and looms for weavers. The perilous economic state of weavers generated grants for purchasing basics such as flour and sugar. Grants also included yarn needed to make the product for which weavers would receive payment. Other poverty-alleviating groups supporting goods made by local villagers included the Scottish Home Industries Association (1889), the Highland Home Industries Association, and the Crofters' Agency. Local women linking tweed to these movements included gentry such as Lady Dunmore, the Duchess of Sutherland and Lady Gordon-Cathcart. Well-meaning patrons of local textiles also included a Mrs. Thomas, Mrs. Mary Stewart Mackenzie and a Mrs. Platt.

The "Arts and Crafts" movement began in the 1860s under the leadership of prominent writers and artists such as John Ruskin and William Morris. Reaction against industrialization's mass production encouraged creation and consumption of locally produced items. Support for items such as hand-woven tweed came from an aesthetic standpoint, beyond sympathy for impoverished rural producers. The underlying notion lay in promoting handmade goods in a variety of materials. Objects ranged from pottery vases and plates to lamps, wallpaper, furniture and textiles. The intent of trendsetters reflected sensibilities favoring pre-modern craft design in the face of homogeneous machine products. Charles Rennie Mackintosh, Scotland's leading proponent, created Art Nouveau with his own designs. The Arts and Crafts movement spread as an international trend in the first decades of the twentieth century. Styles supported furniture makers such as the Stickley brothers in the U.S. and wood block printers in Japan. The cost of time-intensive handmade items relative to factory products limited the market to wealthy consumers. The complexity of the process led to more practical machined shortcuts.

Capital in the textile industry concentrated in the hands of the merchant wholesaler. This sector controlled the mechanical means of production. They served as the sole connection with knowledge of and access to the material market. The merchant supplied yarn as needed by the weaver, rented out the loom, then collected and marketed the weaver's output. In locations like Yorkshire with large concentrations of weavers the workers were more likely to own their own machines and could remain more independent. One of the biggest challenges remained enforcing standards of regularity. The retail market required a predictable product. Lady Dunmore's founding of a training school in Alloa for weavers responded to this concern. From the beginning of Harris Tweed production, Lady Dunmore aimed for a customer base expecting consistently high quality.

Trademark protection with the sign of the orb and Maltese cross certified Harris Tweed since 1903. The Harris Tweed Association's job was to protect the proud and controversially named product. Geographical limitations applied to activities taking place in the Outer Hebrides islands of Lewis, the Uists and Benbecula islands. Harris is combined physically in the Isle of Lewis, named for its larger northern part. The textile was initially defined simply:

"Harris Tweed meant a tweed, hand-spun, hand-woven and dyed by the crofters and cottars in the Outer Hebrides."

The first mill-connected operation in the region was a hydro-powered carding operation in Harris. This popular low-cost form of energy generation characterized the late 18th century Fall Line mills in the United States. By 1903 Lewis' major town of Stornoway also sported Aeneas Mackenzie's carding mill. A waterside slip that formerly supported ship construction and repair activities sponsored by Matheson hosted the carding facility. In 1918 the mill morphed into the Newall and Sons mill. A general merchant in the meat business, Newall accepted tweed as payment for a meat purchase. He reportedly came to appreciate its commodity value. Since the carded wool was ready to twist into yarn, a spinning plant joined the carding facility. It faded after a few years when weavers wanted to keep more of the process literally in their hands.

The Trade Marks Act of 1905 mandated the standardization of an entity to fit the protected description. Tweed merchants around the Outer Hebrides quickly filed to establish their product. Harris Tweed thereby became the first to benefit from a British trademark. Harris merchants saw this as a way of fending off mill spun yarn use in weaving. Goals included keeping another segment of the production process local, standardizing a high-quality affiliation, and getting their geographic affiliation established. The only mills and largest concentration of weavers currently in operation lie on the Lewis section of their shared island.

The time was ripe for industrialization. In 1906 businessman Kenneth Mackenzie started a spinning and carding mill. As Harris Tweed Scotland (formerly Kenneth Mackenzie Ltd.) it is now the largest on Lewis. A subsidiary in Tarbert, the largest village on Harris, dates from Leverhulme's time as Laird of the Isle. Set up as Harris Handwoven Tweed Company, the company was owned by Leverhulme's former Harris factor. This indicates the wealth that men in such a position could accumulate while divesting others of their belongings.

Islanders utilized mainland Scottish as well as Isle of Lewis mills for the laborious process of wool carding and yarn spinning. During the inter-war years of 1914-1934 mainland Scottish mills spun an estimated half of all yarn used in Hebridean products. This enabled a quicker increase in the production of tweed wool fabric. Weaver skill was better invested in production of the prized patterns utilizing numerous color combinations. Hand woven tweed came from islanders' homes, true to the cottage industry tradition. It was now increasingly supplied for outside sale. Small producers met market needs until the inter-World War period, when mainland spun yarn also made the branded fabric. A recognized threat to maintenance of reliable brand quality lay in the removal of spinning to the mills. This resulted in an admixture of non-virgin wool creating the pejoratively termed "Stornoway Tweed" or "Harry's Tweed" marking its lower quality. Mainland mills spun yarn used in Harris Tweed into the 1960s, supplying around 16% of tweed content.

In 1918 canny soap magnate Lord Leverhulme purchased a controlling share of Mackenzie mill stock the same year that he purchased the Isle of Lewis. Harris Tweed clearly held promise as a business venture. His purchase of additional tweed sought to consolidate the industry under his control. Leverhulme's plans to invest his wealth in improvements modernizing his new real estate fared no better than those of his predecessor Matheson. Leverhulme's efforts at promoting efficiency extended to advocating mill spun yarn. This would violate the 1903 trademark definition of Harris Tweed. Such a step lay at the heart of Lewis' tweed's quality threats from inferior adulterated yarn made off the island. By 1924 four spinning mills on Lewis took up slack employment from the demise of Leverhulme's favored but failed herring industry.

Lack of a finishing facility in the Outer Hebrides further removed Harris Tweed from the quality control exercised by local cottage producers. Predictable results came from continued adulterated products. Much more than 'efficiency' was at stake as multi-stage production leaked off-island. Less scrupulous, more mechanized businesses became part of the process. Weaving remained on the looms of locals, but brand quality was increasingly endangered. Some island mills moved into full fabric production, converting their own mill spun yarn into tweed. In 1930 a mill set up in a former canning facility under the direction of former fisherman and tweed commission agent James Macdonald. In the booming 1920s he also wove tweed. Three years after its establishment, Macdonald's mill became the first fully integrated vertical (carding, spinning, finishing) mill on Lewis. Transition during the 1920s- '30s included a growing incidence of mills and independent producers using off-island facilities for various steps of the process. Fifty percent of producers used mainland mill spun yarn, weaving and finishing procedures. This clearly violated Harris Tweed geographic restrictions.

Such practices led in turn to the 1934 Act of Parliament. The legislature strengthened the claim of Outer Hebrides producers to limit the use of Harris Tweed to products from their geographically limited and carefully defined islands. Island spinning mills maintained standards since they were more easily inspected. Another crucial clarification restricted Orb certified fabric to home-loomed output. Looms in individual dwellings were re-installed outside the mills. The 1934 Act clarified that:

> *"Harris Tweed means a tweed made from pure virgin wool produced in Scotland, spun, dyed, and finished in the Outer Hebrides and hand-woven by the islanders at their own homes in the Islands of Lewis, Harris, Uist, Barra and their several pertinences, and all known as the Outer Hebrides."*

A side effect lay in providing an income path for the main population concentration in rural villages on the west coast. Work went to two new small mills with which these mills contracted near the east coast city of Stornoway. Frequent ferries plied the connection over the turbulent Minch waterway. One of the two new mills that sprouted up around this time supplied the first fully integrated tweed operation. Operations included carding, spinning and ultimately finishing the home-woven cloth. The second mill was located in Stornoway, the island's business center but not the center of weaving. The improved Hattersley loom, in use since 1919 but new to Lewis in 1938, provided income for a new source of labor. Disabled servicemen worked in their rural west coast homes to produce more complex patterns at greater speed than they could in the mills. They fed the mills in Stornoway as they recuperated from feeding the wars of Great Britain. In 1946 James Macdonald, one of the authors of the 1934 orb legislation, established a rival mill on the mainland. His Harris Tweed used yarn milled on the wrong side of the Minch. The challenge was on.

Independent producers periodically evaded compliance with the all-Isle restrictions from the time of Lord Leverhulme through the first half of the 20th century. Assisted by merchant wholesalers, small operators used mainland facilities for steps such as yarn spinning and post-weaving finishing. Mills there made a smoother fabric more suitable to some segments of the market. Disputes concerning where what steps could be done continued through the Second World War period. Contention focused on mill spun yarn supplied both from the Scottish mainland and several mills in Stornoway. Simmering disputes ended with a major court case settled by Lord Hunter in 1964 definitively declaring that all steps in the Harris Tweed process must occur only in the islands of the Outer Hebrides (Figure 3.2).

Figure 3.2 Cloth, inspection, single loom, Carloway

Modernization and Textile Transition: Pendleton USA

The move from land-based farm, fishing, herding and husbandry occupations to factory-based manufacturing work occurred in similar stages across rapidly developing economies in geographically disparate locations. Countries experiencing a textile-led industrial revolution ranged from England and the United States to Germany and Japan. General merchants in some cases doubled as independent weavers. They also functioned as middlemen for Harris Tweed producers in much the same way as their Japanese counterparts did at the dawn of the 20th century. This was an unmistakable sign of a developing capitalist economy. Successful entrepreneurial efforts focused on niche specializations serving distinct purposes. Merchants handled tweed orders and delivered mill-spun yard to designated weavers. They also collected the cloth and sent the bundles off for finishing and certification. Merchants finally directed stamped cloth to their destination customers.

In the southwestern United States, wool merchants handled Navajo rug commerce in trading posts. They collected finished product from the weaver in exchange for credit toward purchase of commodity goods in the merchant's store. The weaver's wares were then sold by the merchant to outside contacts, connecting with larger scale markets. Establishment of what became the popular Native American patterned blankets of Pendleton Mill in the U.S. Northwest represents an ironic twist on the Southwest flow of blankets made by Natives to trade to a non-native market. In the Pendleton case blankets made by an American mill were designed for a Native market, later popular across the country for a variety of wool textile products much as Harris Tweed diversified in its fashion applications.

Enterprising English textile weaver Thomas Kay migrated to the mills of New England in the mid-1800s. He left in 1889 to open the second mill in the new state of Oregon's fertile western Willamette Valley (Figure 3.3). His family's fabric would become famous for their adaptations of Native American designs, carrying on the innovation tradition.

Figure 3.3 Bobbin spinning at Kay Mill, 1889

Several other ironies proved keys to Pendleton wool's success. Kay's eldest child was a female. Although the sibling most interested in textile production, Fannie could not inherit the business. She departed the family firm with her retail merchant husband in order to set up a far more successful factory operation in eastern Oregon. The town of Pendleton was well located at a juncture of sheep and shipping via a rare railroad connection. In their first encounters with hungry whites, local Indian tribes hospitably provided food to members of the Lewis and Clark party and later explorers. Trading posts set up in Nez Perce and Umatilla Indian territory in 1812 and 1818 were short-lived. So were the first missionaries (massacred) in the area. By 1893 the first area mill began its operation on 1893. Local tribes were decimated and largely resettled when the mill began producing "Indian blankets" three years later. Traditional Northwest Indian blankets used buffalo hides or a combination of bark and wool from dogs and goats. Production could take from one to two years.

The Bishop family bought Pendleton's shuttered scouring mill in 1909. The town offered financial incentives to support needed employment. A year later a retail store opened, combining Fannie's familiarity with textile production and her husband's merchant acumen. To cater to the local Indian trade a designer consulted with tribes throughout the West on color and pattern preferences. The mill built up friendly relations with a cross-community rodeo that continues to today as the famous Pendleton Round-Up. Retail publicity outreach came in the 1920s with presentation of a "Native American Inspired" blanket to the U.S. President. A popular mail catalog pushed outdoor styles, blankets for the 1932 Olympics, and woolen supplies for the military in World War II.

A second Pendleton mill opened in 1912 at Washougel, Washington along the Columbia River across from Portland, Oregon. It continues as an active mill partner. The Pendleton operation specializes in the more complex "Indian" designs. The first machine added at Washougel was a carding machine in 1930. Wool is currently sent to Texas for carding as part of a typical geographically dispersed production chain. The Texas operation also scours, cleans, and grades the wool, produced by Oregon Rambouillet sheep among other sources. Wool returns to Washougel for the rest of the mechanized process. Machinery from Italy and Germany predominate in the factory. Menswear is made in Mexico; women's wear comes from overseas locations in China, Vietnam, Mexico and Central America. Globally sourced inexpensive labor continues to run the textile mills and spur farm to factory migration building a new international middle class.

Tough Times and Textiles: Early 20th Century China

China marked the turn of the twentieth century with the Boxer Rebellion. A harbinger of turmoil to come, the uprising augured the impending loss of the Qing Dynasty's Mandate of Heaven. The capital of Beijing came under siege by a joint foreign expedition. The aging Manchu dowager empress, last imperial ruler of China, issued a new set of surrenders to foreign demands. She consequently regained her throne and rebuffed the Boxer's demands to "overthrow the Qing, expel the foreigners." The Qing dissolved with the death of the dowager. Foreigners continued to claim parts of the country. A saying at the time likened China to a ripe melon carved up for consumption.

Living in poverty like their Hebridean counterparts, one third of peasant households continued to weave their cloth until the mid-1930s. At that point the majority of Shanghai workers, particularly female migrants, worked in the cotton textile industry. Male silk workers led all other economic sectors in the frequency of their strikes. Mistreatment of factory workers in the Shanghai extraterritorial zone compounded unhappiness with post-World War I arrangements. The resulting 1925 May 30th Movement was a prelude to the Communist revolution two decades later.

The French concession became the birthplace of the Chinese Communist Party in 1927. Extraterritorial French law protected members from arrest by the reigning National Party (Kuomintang, or KMT) under Generalissimo Chiang Kai-chek. Protesting working conditions, weavers formed half of Shanghai's Communist Party leadership. Through the 1940s this cadre proved critical in turning China's largest city into a communist stronghold. Cotton strikes involved much larger numbers of workers than silk weavers. They occurred less frequently, but prompted the banding together of workers in informal unions.

Housing for Chinese factory workers adopted the look of Western row houses. Even trim topping more affluent door frames resembled Western rather than native designs. These aging areas of Shanghai former foreign concessions, known as *lilong,* are largely gone (Figure 3.4). In their place the government created a *lilong* museum to contrast with new apartment tower replacement dwellings, often at a distance from the central high-priced land cleared for commercial development in the workers' New China.

Figure 3.4 Shanghai *lilong* lanes

The end of extraterritoriality left Chinese Communist Party members open to expulsion by KMT-affiliated gangs. In October 1934 Mao's two-year Long March led survivors to the loess wasteland of northern Yenan province. By 1937 the International Labor Organization's World Textile Conference had heard many complaints of worker exploitation in China's foreign concession zones. Consequent appeals asked for their intercession to apply international rules for the protection of workers in China. Their concern contains a contemporary resonance with worker complaints in the current globalization era. Japan's invasion of China in 1938 temporarily spared the foreign concession areas of treaty port cities until war with the U.S. broke out in December 1941. The communist's People's Liberation Army waged successful, classic guerrilla warfare against first the Japanese invaders and later the KMT. Defeated Nationalists fled to the nearby island of Taiwan with what remained of their military. Many industrialists, including Shanghai's textile barons, accompanied them. A new China rose from ashes of conflicts, but that would take almost half a century. How China survived two civil wars (Nationalist vs. Communist plus the Cultural Revolution) and foreign invasions to become a 21st century global economic powerhouse is a truly amazing story. The tale holds lessons for other emerging countries, seeking to retain significant parts of their culture and self-identity in the process.

CHAPTER 4

Asian Textile Transitions: Modernization Mixes

"Technology was the missing link that was the key to the successful transition to mechanized production, allowing this ... industry to spearhead Japan's industrialization. At the same time the developments of the 1880s initiated a longer term technological and management trajectory which would facilitate the spate of company mergers that characterized cotton production from the turn of the century, and led to its international success and domination by a few very large concerns." Janet Hunter, "Reviving the Kansai Cotton Industry"

"Japan loves color, and loves to be reactive with color and fabrics – their consumers also really appreciate provenance and craftsmanship." Margaret Ann Macleod, Brand Director Harris Tweed Hebrides

Colonial Influences

Britain played an outsized role in global textile manufacturing. Its nineteenth century position as an industrialization pioneer began with textiles. Britannia also ruled the waves as a major colonizer, extending an empire throughout Asia. Those who tried to resist the latter needed to adopt the former. Japan's rise as East Asia's first industrial powerhouse, during neighbor China's dismemberment, illustrates this path. By the mid-19th century non-Western textile mills appeared in Britain's colony of India. Two decades later Japan's Tomioka mill complex exported its machine-made textiles too. The offshore island chain desperately sought to stave off imperial inroads made by Britain in its conquest of increasing parts of mainland Asia. Demands for material generated by World War I and during the recovery aftermath speeded textile production. In China textile production concentrated in the Westernizing extraterritorial parts of Shanghai. In Japan, cloth production took place primarily in the business center of Osaka. India's industry withered as colonial master England protected its Manchester mills. Booming Bombay was relegated to supplying the local market with lower quality goods. Imperial domination of productive colonies seemed an ideal industrialization engine feeding on submissive low-cost labor. It became a fuse with a long smoldering taper.

Key industries such as steel supplied construction material for industry-supportive infrastructure. In the interest of managing its colonial "jewel in the crown," Britain built India's "Grand Trunk Line." This route still serves as a major rail backbone transporting people and goods across the subcontinent. Japan utilized native labor and finance. This resulted in transferable skills to other mechanized industries such as textiles. It also kept scarce capital in the country. India's cotton textile industry remained suppressed by Britain's dominance. One of Mahatma Gandhi's self-sufficiency campaigns championed reverting to home spinning looms. India's global giant Reliant Industry came from the post-independence switch to synthetic fabrics. This company plays a role at a later stage in our story. Japan's industrialization era textile industry flourished with the manufacture and export of silk and cotton at new Western-modeled mills, as seen in the next section.

Japan's Journey: Tradition and Textiles

The nation of Japan consists of four major islands plus the Ryukyu chain to the south. Isolated outposts include the disputed Kiril islands still under Russia's post-World War II control. Japan's total land area is slightly smaller than the state of California. The United Kingdom consists of one major island, the northern part of Ireland, and several island clusters including the Inner and Outer

Hebrides. Total land area is slightly smaller than California's northern neighbor, the state of Oregon. The UK contains half the population of Japan and is 2/3rds the size of Japan.

Both of these island nation-states are poised beside a large continent whose countries they sporadically contended with over a long time span of wary co-existence. Both countries also maintain a distinctive culture with its own language, literature, religion, customs and clothes. Particular affinities of Japan with the Outer Hebrides form key parts of a story used in marketing Harris Tweed. They also explain the textile's appeal to upwards of 90% of the current tweed market exported to this one small country. Similarities include a rugged landscape, cold northern climate, predominant settlement in small village clusters, and strong ties of allegiance to small family/clan groups. Both are battle-tested survivors of adversity in many forms. Japanese interest in provenance – the aspect of historical belonging to a place – is also a characteristic shared with Hebrideans, and helps to explain the attraction of Harris Tweed. An identifiable source for the product rests in the exact weaver who wove the roll of fabric. Records list the maker's name along with the mill for which they worked and the cloth's precise color and pattern composition.

Mills played a key role as the leading sector in Japan's rapid industrialization. Modernization advanced by selectively emulating Western practices. The appeal of Harris Tweed to an affluent and fashionable segment of contemporary Japan is better understood in the context of cultural and historical perceptions. Class implications adhere to this material expression of a once humble cloth chosen for leisurewear by gentry and royalty. The respect within Japanese society for crafts people pursuing a traditional art form expressed in a textile continues as a cultural core in that country. Japanese see hand-hewn crafts as an important symbol of a unique identity. Master crafts people fashioning historically important cultural items, from pottery to swords, are recognized as icons and honored by the state. Alan Bain, former owner of Carloway Mill, recognized this characteristic fit, declaring that "If Harris Tweed were a

Japanese product it would have been declared a national treasure, and . . . both promoted and protected."

Silk served as the wrap of the traditional Japanese elite. As was China's practice, silk was cultivated in that country since the Bronze Age. The rural poor masses made do with cotton and vegetal fiber homespun material such as hemp and ramie (*asa*). The latter were locally grown and processed by women working on their own spinning wheels. Rural weavers in western countries were in a similar situation. Japan imported cotton fabric from China and India prior to the 15th century, then later obtained seeds to grow it as a domestic crop. Finished cotton fabric from the main island of Kyushu sold throughout the country. Spinning and weaving served as a cottage industry for home and small local markets. During the pre-industrial era (prior to 1868) production drew on a countrywide network of material suppliers, weavers, dyers, finishers, and distributors.

Traditional colors made from natural dyes featured blue, black and grey. Embroidery was stitched on hemp and cotton patchwork material. Natural dyes taken from local flora adorned fabrics. A distinctive reddish-brown color, for example, came from persimmons and mosquito netting featured blue indigo, seen as helping to repel insects. This use of color remains a selling point romanticized by contemporary Harris Tweed producers as an embodiment of their islands' physical and esthetic essence. The weave known in Japan as *zanshi* uses lumpy mixed color threads woven in squared patterns; the textured effect is similar to Scottish tweed. Cloth known as *banshi ori*, produced since the 1790s, features a process of dyeing and weaving on large looms. The finished nubby cloth sports small patterns including multi-colored checks. Other resemblances of this cloth to contemporary Harris Tweed include its use in home interiors, furnishings and female clothing. Such resonances may well have paved the path for Japanese acceptance of an alien cloth that became strikingly popular.

The Meiji Revolution: Opening to the West

Throughout most of its history Japan sought to isolate itself from the outside world. A notable exception was Japan's opening to Chinese influence during the Tang Dynasty (618-907 CE). Japan adopted a version of Chinese characters to indicate Chinese-derived words. A form of the Buddhist religion was later modified to Japanese Zen, an interpretation derived from the Chinese Chan School. Tang Dynasty female dress became the kimono. Imperial power was secondary to that of the warlords. The Tokugawa shogun's shift of the country's capital to the former village of Edo on the opposite side of Honshu in 1603 signified the power shift. Local rulers commuted between the imperial court in Kyoto and the new shogun-constructed city of Tokyo.

Mid-19th century Japan did not fail to notice the ominous military incursions of advanced Western countries such as Great Britain. Demands of would-be colonizers featured trade access and extraterritorial acquisitions for itself and allies France, Germany, and the United States. The 1860 arrival of Admiral Matthew Perry's coal-fired "black ships" from a little-known country across the vast Pacific Ocean inspired widespread trepidation. Japan resolved not to go the disastrous route of China, in a saying of the time being "carved up like a ripe melon".

Powerful and enterprising Japanese officials surreptitiously sent a few college students to enroll in U.S. colleges while it was still illegal to leave the country. The task of these hard-working students in the late Tokugawa shogunate (1603-1867) was to save their country by learning what made the West so strong. Rutgers University posthumously granted the first PhD awarded to a Japanese student in the U.S. The doctoral candidate perished from illness aggravated by overwork before the degree could be conferred. "Big guns, fast ships" became the motto of the 1868 Meiji Revolution (*meiji* means "enlightened"). Meiji leaders re-prioritized and elevated the power position of the young Emperor over the old shogun-led samurai class. Military strength remained a priority, switching from hand-produced swords to machine-produced guns and cannon. Technology adoption led the way, from "fire vehicle" coal-powered trains on "iron road" tracks to modern ships, Western-style clothes, and leisure class skills from piano playing to golf. At the same time, Japanese farmers sustained their livelihood by producing both rice and silk. One met demand for food, the other fed the new textile mills.

Japan also produced late-19th century tweed for its home market. Elites sought approval for the country's industrial prowess, along with following fashions of the developed world. By the 21st century Japan formed a major market for the orb-stamped Harris Tweed authentic goods. The leading Asian modernizer since the Meiji reforms, Japan spearheaded its drive to industrialization through the use of largely female textile workers. Two of the earliest enterprises were the Tomioka Silk Filature Mill, funded and managed by the national government in 1872, and the Osaka Spinning Mill in 1882. Located north of Tokyo, Tomioka used silk reeling technology from France. The mills clustered around Osaka, the new business center of Japan, concentrated on cotton technology borrowed from England.

A new form of budding entrepreneurial capitalism led these enterprises: the family-headed conglomerate known as *zaibatsu*. These were later called *keiretsu* when oligopolies were technically abolished after World War II. The successful formula of concentrated monopoly power was hard to forsake as an efficient tool for concentrating scarce capital in trusted family hands. A key step relevant to what was about to happen to Harris Tweed production on the Isle of Lewis, another isolated island floating offshore of a mainland manufacturing power, lay in the role of business-savvy network builders:

> ". . . regional merchant-manufacturers used their [traditional textile] business, a typical example of incrementally developed local manufacturing, to support the introduction of mechanized cotton spinning factories whose output eventually had to be sold outside the region to achieve economies of scale. This transition from local to national markets

illustrates how merchants led the local industrial revolutions . . . [by taking] some of what they learned from the new textile mills and used it to modernize the technology and organization of *kasuri* weaving "
Nakamura 2015, p.23

The industrial revolution in Scotland and Great Britain was well established by the 1850s. The leadership role taken by major producers and local firms in transitioning to production by machinery within a factory remains controversial. By the late 1880s textile production was the main rural industry in Japan. Local merchant-manufacturers coordinated traditional *kasuri* textile weaving and dyeing. Much like the tweed production system of the Hebrides, dealers furnished home weavers with hand-spun thread and in return collected the cottage industry-produced woven cloth. Thread spinning suppliers were the first to industrialize as a factory company, seeking to increase cloth production to meet demand. Further standardization of production came through organizing a subcontracting system to supply consistent colors and quality of material. An electricity company was created for a reliable supply of energy used to mechanize twining and knotting. This critical infrastructure led to the step-by-step migration of textile production from home to mill.

By the early 1900s textile production in Japan reached European levels. Silk, wool and cotton manufacture was the country's most important industry in the first decades of the twentieth century. Textile factories employed one-third of the Japanese workforce through the early 1940s. Women laboring long hours for low pay in cottage and small workshop conditions represented the majority of employees in this industry. This was a globally common situation for textiles. In 1919 Japan produced wool worth almost 122 million yen. By 1925 this rose to 185 million yen worth of fabric, and reached the level of almost 1,154 million yen worth of output in 1981. Wool was an increasingly popular fabric in the Japanese market. Its design became a matter of international competition to clothe a growing middle class.

By 1920 Japan produced its own version of mislabeled Harris Tweed. This by-product of global popularity contributed to the 1933 Act of Parliament clarifying and reasserting the definition of Hebridean-produced Harris Tweed and the signifying role of the Orb trademark. The Act laid the groundwork for receptivity to a reconfigured Harris Tweed introduced back to Japan in the early 21st century. A new age of global openness re-imaged retro-metro products spanning and merging historical eras and place allusions. Classic black and white herringbone patterns remain popular, but bright colors such as orange and pink in a lighter weight fabric attract young Japanese wearers of Harris Tweed.

Popular Japanese gifts feature expensive, recognizable brand name products. Best bets are items easy to bring back in a suitcase from a trip abroad or ship over a long distance without breaking. All these features fit Harris Tweed. The cloth is marketed in Japan as an enduring investment. Appeal is enhanced with its gentry connected history of being made by hand on another small, struggling and somewhat isolated, distinctive island. Tweed's many uses translate into "Hello Kitty" designs, teddy bears, teacups, stationary, and Japanese retro manga costumes. They also, more traditionally, feature in "Japan Fashion Week" runway offerings.

According to the Brand Director of Harris Tweed Hebrides, the Japanese love of and appreciation for striking colors and fabrics, combined with an interest in quality craftsmanship and production history, make Harris Tweed a very attractive fit with the Japanese market. Retailers of tweed products join British government-sponsored "Buy British" campaigns to exhibit their wares and attract buyers during Asian exhibitions. The often-positive resulting partnerships help ease the way for Harris Tweed's introduction into a new market needing native middlemen.

Thailand: Jim Thompson Silk

The Thai Silk Company Limited, co-founded in 1948 by Americans George Barrie and Jim Thompson, transformed the making and marketing of a classic Thai textile spun by women working on small looms in their home. The onset of a cold war followed the tumult of a world war. Migrants from China long ago mingled with older occupants of this Southeast Asian peninsula. Incomers brought with them knowledge of silkworm cultivation and how to weave their threads into a lustrous fabric. As colorful and noted as his silk, Thompson sported many titles. He was the son of a well-to-do U.S. textile magnate/architectural designer. He was also a member of the military and a secret agent of the Office of Strategic Services, precursor to the CIA. As a specialist in Southeast Asia, Thompson's final affiliation fueled speculation that this may have contributed to his mysterious disappearance in Malaysia's remote Cameron Highlands while taking an unaccompanied hike on vacation. His father's occupation may have influenced the son's work at the time, creating a new outlet for Thai textile handicrafts.

Jim Thompson Silk transformed an iconic native textile into a global industry. The company provided a home-based livelihood for many poor Thai females. From the early 1950s to the early 1970s it was a leading export of the country. When Thompson became aware of Thai silk only a few knowledgeable in the craft remained. Weavers concentrated in an area across from the *klong* (canal) where Thompson built his art museum-like house. Now a tourist destination, the dwelling preserves a large collection of traditional Thai pottery, statuary, and other under-valued craft items. Although Thai silk manufacture became an all-mill operation, Thompson demonstrated a marketing knack by using a popular array of brightly colored jewel tones. This range resembles the palette now favored by Japanese consumers. As a step to supplant illegal but profitable drug cultivation in obscure highland areas, the Queen supported retail shops featuring more licit cottage industry products. Offerings range from canned foods to cloth accessories and anything else that can be hand produced for an affluent local and international market. Thompson's breakthrough silk showed how housebound women could supply a global export demand. Working on traditional looms, they produced quality fabric in forms responsive to a larger market.

The notion that cottage-based participation by native weavers could lead to a world-famous product echoes in contemporary Harris Tweed. Both silk and wool textiles feature hues resonant with an Asian clientele. Several of Thompson's innovations were also reminiscent of key breakthroughs in the evolution of Harris Tweed. Introduction of chemical dyes simplified the process of natural plant-based colorings. Designs are tailored for uses needed by a global/Western market. Introduction of the outcome to a coterie of h fashionable peers in New York City built a bridge pioneered by Harris' Lady Dunmore.

Bhutan: Royal Intervention

> *Weaving is an integral component of the culture and tradition of Bhutan. With the aim to preserve and promote this living art, the Royal Textile Academy of Bhutan was instituted in May 2005 under the patronage of Her Majesty Ashi Sangay Choden Wangchuck as a non-government, non-profit organization. It will be established as an educational center for the training of individuals in the traditional art of weaving, thereby preserving and conserving the culture of Bhutanese Textiles.* The Royal Textile Academy of Bhutan, Myers and Bean, 1994

Bhutan survives as a small former kingdom located in the Himalayas. It is surrounded by a protective India, an expansive China, and threatened by near-neighbor Nepal's demographic overflow. A popular Bhutanese lament for their situation refers to the nation as "a yam between two boulders." Bhutan draws on its Buddhist beliefs to navigate the perils of their geography and a development level exacerbated by mountainous isolation. The government promotes a "Middle Path" between clinging to a traditional past or accelerating into an uncertain modern future. Its economic policy attempts to measure "Gross National Happiness" (GNH) rather than a materialistic Gross National Product, which in Bhutan's case is not particularly high. Measurement of GNH is based on the "Four Pillars" of 1) cultural and 2) environmental preservation, 3) good governance, and 4) balanced and equitable human development. Such aspirations pose a tall order indeed, but became globally distinctive. Bhutan's development landscape is clear in Figure 4.1. One side of the river continues to practice terraced agriculture. The other side shows modern structures of a new cement-heavy small city. A tenuous bridge links both sides.

Figure 4.1 Urban and rural sides of development

Bhutan's traditional textiles feature as one of the "Thirteen Arts and Crafts" targeted for government support and preservation. Pieces sport an array of bright colors and embroidered designs displaying motifs from its Buddhist faith in traditional patterns. Real and mythical flying beasts represent emblems from ancient folk tales. All lend their unique cultural stamp to the cloth handwoven by Bhutanese women on distinctive traditional looms. Interest in and sponsorship of the textile craft by nobility and members of the royal household have historic roots. Credit goes to a former king's sister for introducing the Tibetan triangular shaped horizontal loom in the 1930s. Fixed or framed, similar looms come from neighboring India. Other types of looms used for Bhutanese cloth include the card loom and the backstrap loom derived from Indian or Southeast Asian models. The most talented weavers practiced at the royal looms close to the palace compound. They produced a higher grade of intricately embroidered cloth than that used for everyday clothes or for partial tax credit. Cotton and silk are the basic materials used in the colorful cloth, usually covered with embroidery. Native yak and sheep provide locally sourced wool threads.

Queen Mother Ashi Sonam Choden Wangchuck set up The Tarayana Foundation in 1971. One of its primary functions is to promote Bhutanese traditional crafts including textiles. In the mid-1980s two books by American collectors of the exotic textiles brought the Bhutanese crafts an enthusiastic world reception. Applications of the material to global market-oriented goods include tableware, bed covers, eyeglass cases, and accessories such as purses and shawls. They are designed for a deliberately slowly developing tourist market (Figure 4.2). Encouraging cottage industries serve another goal of the royal rulers: keeping modernization controlled and discouraging rural to urban migration. Its purpose was to avoid the many ills obvious to observers of the developing world by that time. Proceeds from the sale of their fabric were intended to go into the hands of the women weavers. This supplemented the family income, providing food, school clothes and books for their children. As in the Outer Hebrides, schools are now required to teach the indigenous language along with English. This represents an attempt to preserve the Dzongkha language as a written as well as spoken culturally rich communication form.

Royal patronage established the National Textile Museum to showcase artifacts important to Bhutan's cultural heritage in 2001. Partial funds come from public and private grants by various countries and individuals. The structure is located close to the national library and an example of a traditional farmhouse. The style and function are a folkways lesson for future generations in an inevitably urbanizing society. Textile production by hand takes

Figure 4.2 Bhutanese traditional fabrics and designs

place as an integral part of cultural identity. New designs for a global market maintain traditional skills. The domestic market for Bhutanese cloth remains supported by the 1989 law of "One Nation, One People." Requirements mandate the wearing of traditional Bhutanese clothes by all citizens as a sign of their communal affiliation. All building must be constructed using traditional elements of style. The original function may have vanished, but national identity assertion is visual.

Bhutan's approach to textile production represents one end of the spectrum of tradition maintenance. Lack of more mechanized industrial alternatives led to reliance on royal and foreign sponsorship support to continue cottage industry production. While a colorful foreigner resuscitated Thai silk and preserved the work of native weavers, Thailand's silk manufacture commercialized to modern mill production. Scotland's Hebridean Harris Tweed process seeks an evolving "Middle Way", to use a Buddhist phrase employed in both Bhutan and Thailand. The ideal balance might situate between an all-mill process that attempts to replicate the quality of traditional Thai silk, and the Bhutanese situation of deliberately delayed modernization implementation. Forces of globalization demand high quality along with low cost rapid production. This occurs even with unique items representing a distinctive national niche. Global markets apply relentless pressure to transform everything that makes traditional textile significant. How can that balance be struck and stick?

CHAPTER 5

Crossing Paths: Scottish Crofters, Chinese Industrialization

"It has to be recognized that the Harris Tweed industry is dying. Radical action has to be taken . . . The world is no longer beating a path to our door." Harris Tweed Association Chairman, 1990

"China must cross the river by feeling for the stones with our feet . . . It doesn't matter whether a cat is black or white, as long as it catches mice." Deng Xiaoping, late 1980s

Textiles led the Industrial Revolution, and were the first industry to suffer from the enormous effects of the globalization transformation. With a huge ambitious workforce and gigantic potential market, China was long the elephant (or dragon) in the room in regard to global production agreements designed to delay the competitive impacts of the developing world on developed world producers and laborers. Preceded by a similar arrangement in 1962, the Multi-Fiber Arrangement (MFA) set the textile industry's terms of engagement from 1973 until the lifting of import quotas in 2005. Developed world retailers and consumers rejoiced, anticipating less expensive clothing; for developed world manufacturers, there was less cause for jubilation.

Demonstrating the rapidity and extent of its manufacturing takeoff, China zoomed from producing 4% of global clothing exports in 1980, when Deng Xiaoping's political-economic reforms began, to one-fourth of total global clothing exports two decades later. China's peasants particularly found the low skill level of factory textile production amenable for a first step into industrialized labor and an urban centered cash economy. This situation mirrored that of labor's leap from farm to factory in previous development take-offs experienced in 19th century Europe and North America. Although the substitution of capital-intensive machinery tends to depress the number of workers involved, an increase in higher profit work in a variety of textile applications outside clothing keeps the demand for laborers from diminishing greatly. Examples of innovative textile applications beyond initial cloth production include making material for upholstered furniture, accessories, and shoes.

A "race to the bottom" seeking low cost producing areas is too simplistic a concept to encompass all considerations made by companies reallocating the geography of textile work. Due to the predominance of cost considerations, clothing tends to be produced in widely scattered locations by a largely low paid contingent of female workers operating in unattractive conditions. Target market segments in a highly niche-sensitive fashion industry also play a large role in this buyer-focused enterprise. Specialized brands such as Harris Tweed carry a cache that aspiring potential purchasers seek to be associated with, but even bespoke brands are far from immune to forces in the world of fashion and historical associations. Regional production assemblages such as the one discussed in the following sections include Asian textile giants from India to Japan, gathering forces for forays into troubled segments of the developed and drooping regions of Europe.

China Reborn

Victorious Chairman Mao Zedong announced the birth of the People's Republic of China (PRC) from atop the main gate of Tiananmen Square on October 1, 1949. The new communist government quickly assumed management of textile mills as former owners fled to the Kuomintang's (KMT) refuge of the Republic of China on the offshore island of Taiwan. Communism's founding father Karl Marx wrote his *Manifesto* in 1848 at a period of intermittent political revolutionary protest against the industrial revolution's redistribution of economic wealth and power. A small elite of wealthy capitalists were seen as oppressing their workers through extracting undue profit from the uncompensated sweat of the toiling masses. Since textile mills were the first factories to industrialize, and noted for their employment of women and children, the Chinese Communist Party's well-known hostility to this group largely concentrated in Shanghai. As the most Western-influenced historical treaty port city in the country, the Changjiang Delta metropolis was a bastion of leftist influence that inspired the exodus of factory owners to safety elsewhere.

Traditional small-scale rural production of textiles also came to an end. Productive efforts in general consolidated under government control. Employees assigned to a work unit (*danwei*) received their housing, all benefits and place-aligned identity card (*hukou*) through their communal affiliation with their employer. Links were so tight that employees clustered around their specific job site. Giant state-owned enterprises (SOE) provided meals, childcare, and many other life support mechanisms. Huge factories generated mass-produced mechanized loomed production in state-owned mills. This set-up prevailed throughout the disruptive Great Proletarian Cultural Revolution from 1967-1976. The only major location shift of major economic activities occurred during the "Third Line" movement in 1964. This strategy was a defensive reaction to the ongoing Vietnam War and long-simmering fears of a potential U.S.-sponsored invasion by KMT military forces from Taiwan. PRC planners pushed critical production facilities from vulnerable coastal areas to inland locations in western and central China. Textile production joined military units, technology and related facilities from hospitals to universities in the inland migration that often duplicated facilities in coastal regions, but at a safer distance from any possible Taiwan-based invasion.

The 1976 passing of Chairman Mao and the death of his allied military general Lin Biao brought the Party-sponsored "Cultural Revolution" to an end after what is now termed "the lost decade" of the mid- '60s – mid-70s. The highly disruptive period can be seen as the denouement of what was called a "century of humiliation" and civil war. The colorful Deng Xiaoping was brought back from exile in a rural factory to lead the economic revival of China as its "paramount leader", building on his earlier empirical rather than ideological approach to economic restructuring. As a teenager setting sail for France on a mission similar to that of his future mentor and later Prime Minister Zhou Enlai, Deng reportedly told his father that his goal was similar to that of reformers of the previous century: "To learn knowledge and truth from the West in order to save China." A large part of his recipe to "save China" involved experimenting with economic approaches unfettered by ideology and pursuing whatever yielded good results. Some of his most famous sayings are enigmatically articulated in the quotes heading this chapter, using allusions familiar to Chinese skilled in the safety of reading "between the lines".

The resulting post-1978 market reforms greatly affected China's textile industries. An experimental attempt to encourage new thinking that could accelerate China's economic takeoff resulted in the "Township and Village Enterprise" (TVE) movement. This scheme transferred some textile production equipment and functions from the large state-owned enterprises (SOE) to the intermediate-sized and presumably more efficient local facilities. Demise of the TVE structure in the 1980s, following various wasteful attempts relying on ill-prepared "Just Do It" ideas, resulted in looms being appropriated by households for home-centered production. Weaving shifted back to a more traditional small-scale cottage setting with formal introduction of the "household responsibility system". Introduction of bonus incentives fired up traditional textile areas in Hebei, Jiangsu, and Zhejiang. The latter two provinces are conveniently close to the former textile center of Shanghai.

By the 1980s textile production was one of the most highly globalized industries, similar to its pioneering role in the industrial revolution. This was due principally to the relatively low skill-low pay level of its workforce and its highly mechanized (thus readily substitutable of labor for machinery) nature. Historical shifts trace the movement of this industry's production core from the British Isles to North America, from the U.S. northeast to the southeast, and across the Pacific to Japan, the Four Tigers (Taiwan, South Korea, Hong Kong and Singapore), China, and back to the (Central) Americas in a process called re-hemispherization.

The unifying theme in this migration lies with a core to periphery flow, variously termed the "new international division of labor" (NIDL) leading to "hollowing out" and "deindustrialization" in the former core(s). The NIDL spread ideally reflects where in the world labor cost and skills, combined with transportation considerations such as speed and cost plus government incentives, best address competitive manufacturing needs. Areas "hollow out" when formerly core companies leave for more competitive and thus profitable locations. "Deindustrialization" occurs when manufacturing jobs depart and workers need to acquire new jobs, usually in the service sector, moving from machinery to McDonalds, for example. "Off-shore sourcing" refers to the practice of having parts of a product made or assembled outside the major market country. This strategy greatly assisted China's economic rise. Policy makers sagely designed China's economy to feature export-led industrialization and learning by doing various stages in a global commodity production chain.

The next chapter discusses the effect of this strategy on the textile industry as it globalized across various Asian locations and countries. The trajectory of production maturation began with Chinese workers making parts for foreign transnational companies (TNC) in a process called Original Equipment Manufacturing (OEM). Following familiarity with the product and facility in parts production, the next step was Own Design Manufacturing (ODM) involving the major company subcontracting a new product with various defining features to be made abroad. The final step in maturation would be Own Brand manufacturing (OBM) with the formerly near-anonymous parts maker finally graduating into its own company with its own trademark name. The penultimate step, discussed in the following chapter, involves a company in the "developing country" acquiring a part interest in or purchasing an older company in a more developed country through a joint venture or merger and acquisition (M&A) procedure. All of these steps occurred in the textile industry, but in only one case (so far) for the elaborately trademark protected and geographically circumscribed Harris Tweed.

The chronological arc of China's textile industry in the second half of the 20th century thus began with the shift from large and small private settings to very large state owned production facilities from the 1950s through late 1970s. Experiments with various forms of "petty capitalism" (small activities leading to a small scale accumulation of capital, such as selling home-raised eggs or home-based restaurants) began in the 1980s. This led to industrial capitalism under the "market socialism" system prevalent by the early 21st century. A tricky phase, the transition combined the most successful and globally competitive State Owned Enterprise (SOE) facilities with smaller surviving profit-generating units. Textile companies generally adopt a large production - low cost model. The initial flush of industrialization success pulled textile manufacturing in a steady westward direction from its roots in industrial England to the northeast and later (1920s-1970s) southeast U.S., and on to east coast Chinese clusters by the turn of the 21st century. Textiles became the leading edge of China's identity as the "global factory". A new middle class rose from fields to factories in its wake.

The textile industry was heavily influenced by Chinese government policy due to its important ability to employ large numbers of low skilled workers. An example of this effect lies with its mirroring of government development strategy regarding the geographic location needing either starting or accelerating. Textile production historically began in the southeast along the coast of large rivers, utilizing water power and suitable climatic features. In the early years of the communist regime a policy of spreading development more equitably held sway. Textile factories developed in central plains cities such as Xi'an, Xianyang and Zhengzhou as well as the capital region of Beijing-Tianjin and traditional strongholds in southeast coast Shanghai and the Pearl River delta.

Prioritization of development in the most globally competitive locations characterized the "Opening Up" period of the

1980s. This decade saw textile factories thrive and re-concentrate in the southeast. opportunities for export presented by China's acceptance into the WTO at the beginning of the 21st century presented new export opportunities for textile production that quickly took off. The transition also coincided with a political policy aimed to redistribute regions of economic strength. The goal was to stem the huge migration movement of the preceding decades from the more impoverished agricultural areas of central and western China surging to the southeast industrial parks. New textile and apparel factories sprung up in these "sending regions", especially in response to the 2008 global financial downturn.

The government pursued a multi-pronged strategy. The immediate remedy for a downturn was to pump more money into the economy. Another aspect lay with encouraging former migrants to now downscaled east coast factories to seek new jobs in large cities closer to their home districts. Five coastal provinces traditionally strong in textile production – Jiangsu, Zhejiang, Guangdong, Shandong, and Fujian – improved their facilities due in part to pre-existing and improved infrastructure linkages and farsighted leadership. Shandong Ruyi, a company that will feature in the story of Harris Tweed's globalization, falls into this category. It responded to the Premier's call to "Develop the West" by setting up a branch overseas in 2006 in addition to its strong position in its east coast home province.

A hollowing out of Chinese facilities similar to what earlier afflicted developed countries threatens Chinese textiles manufacturers still reliant on an inefficient SOE model. Their associated workers, long benefitting from a state guaranteed safety net, suffer from the dissolution of these "white elephant" behemoths. A more capitalist core of docile (frequently female) rural migrants eager to be off the farm replaces them in more competitive firms. Jobs are often allied with developed world ventures and markets to generate the next organization model – learning, as Deng forecast, by doing and pursuing what works. Such ventures use a Chinese term discussed in the next chapter as a turtle leaping into the ocean overseas.

Lewis Emerges from the Wars

The strategy of employing excess male population as soldiers, diverting them from becoming restive residents with more time than money on their hands, has a long tradition in the Highlands. One example stretches back to Britain's creation of the Seaforth Regiment under Matheson's predecessor as owner of Lewis and Harris, Lord Seaforth. Recruitment posters of tartan-clad brawny lads advertised that serving as a soldier was an honorable manly outlet. This portrayal was particularly attractive since the highlands and islands struggled economically to support an increasing population.

The post-WW II years saw a surge in Harris Tweed's popularity through its application to women's fashion. By the mid-1950s busy looms clacked throughout the islands, with weavers working for piece rate pay. Large vans and land rovers delivered yarn from, and picked up woolen cloth for delivery back to, the mills contracting the home-based weavers. New applications ranged from tailored jackets reminiscent of the fabric's earliest use in menswear, to brightly colored dresses, handbags, and a variety of other cloth items that now used Harris Tweed. By 1947 tweed production reached a peak at 5 million yards, before the industry was undercut by an ill-advised 66.6% tax on hand woven Harris Tweed. Production steadily declined from 1948's 4.46 million yards to 1949's 4.1 million, 1950's 3.78, and 1951's 2.8 million. Output rose back up to 5 million yards in 1954 with a slight recovery in the intervening years, followed by increased production through the early 1960s.

A line in a letter from the Secretary of the Harris Tweed Association in 1949 summed up one of two underlying ongoing issues when he stated, "The over-riding factor which everyone concerned in the Industry must accept as a common basis is quality." The challenge to Harris Tweed from off-island produced non-Orb stamped imitators increased and endangered the cloth's popularity due to anticipatable quality differences. The second major ongoing industry challenge lay in limiting the geography of Harris Tweed's production. Establishment of the organized "Independent Harris Tweed Producers" in 1958 acted as a rival conduit for production steps to take place in non-Isles facilities, from Scotland to global textile centers. The price of Orb-stamped twist yarn from island facilities was felt to be uncompetitive, given the machined methods available elsewhere.

Controversy crested in a 1964 court case, the longest running legal action on the Hebrides. The outcome ruling resulted in Lord Hunter's landmark "*Report*" which ultimately and finally supported the requirement that all Harris Tweed-designated production must remain on the previously defined Hebridean islands in order to earn the mark of the Orb. Lews Castle College opened a new program to train young would-be weavers in the trade – and more importantly imbue them as well with modern work ethics of timeliness in production in order to meet global product demand. The usual mixture of activities - including fine weather for peat cutting, a run of fishing, tending croft crops or sheep needs - would not suffice as a reason to delay weaving deadlines. An additional question concerned whether Harris Tweed weavers should be considered self-employed or employees of Harris Tweed mills, thus entitled to employee benefits commensurate with those of on-site mill employees. They remained, as originally, independent producers free to choose which mill's work they took on and what outlet they otherwise supplied their wool to for final product production and ongoing market sales.

The post-war UK textile industry in general failed to literally capitalize on its Industrial Revolution era primacy, relying instead on aging equipment and approaches. Textile production originally concentrated in British cities such as Lancashire due to its damp climate, considered conducive to thread processing. Access to water for power supply and transportation for shipping also ranked highly. The flow of textiles trended increasingly one way: in favor of imports. Erecting the usual tariff walls and quota restrictions through the Multi Factor Agreement (MFA) bought time but not the transforming rethinking and restructuring needed. Manufacturing in general fell out of favor in its homeland. Eventually the value-added answer of high tech textiles seemed the best response. The ancient cottage industry of Harris Tweed posed another avenue with high profit possibilities, little recognized in the fog of (trade) war.

An Industry on Life Support

The demand slump tweed experienced in the 1970s led to predictable mergers of small firms into larger survivors. Most looms were at least 20 years old, operated largely by weavers relying on their wares for the majority of their income, and longing for better income returns on their time. The major island mills in 1972 were Kenneth Mackenzie Ltd (Stornoway), Tod Holdings Ltd, and Kenneth MacLeod (Shawbost) Ltd. In the five years from 1970 to 1975 tweed production halved. Beginning with mergers in 1972, collapsing mills congealed into "the KM Group" of Kenneth Mackenzie mills, both Stornoway and Shawbost-affiliated, in 1991. Traditional mills such as Mackenzie functioned as middlemen, passing basic production material such as yarn from a mill to its affiliated weavers. These then sent the cottage-woven cloth back to the mill for finishing, certifying and sending to a market for sale.

The 1970s also saw a battle with power-driven mainland mills using some Harris yarn to produce "Hebridean Tweed" minus the orb trademark but responding to a market demand. In 1984 a short-lived boomlet in tweed production preceded a cyclical bust. By 1990 this led to dumping the unwanted surplus on a cut-rate U.S. market. A major battle between weavers and other parts of the industry involved proposed legislation in 1976 for adoption of double-width power looms. Weavers resoundingly rejected this injection of machined modernization, as the conservative "Lewismen" had often reacted to past attempts to change their livelihood conditions in the Matheson-Leverhulme era.

At the same time, markets in Asia were developing, particularly featuring the newly wealthy Japanese. One success marker concerned recognition by domestic government authorities that Harris Tweed was a significant craft industry with a future that deserved and needed protective cultivation. Significant competition came online in the 1990s due to cost and time saving from synthetic fiber and new technologically improved textile machinery. Government-backed investment spurred the debut of low labor cost segment in Asia as a clothing market rival at the lower and middle range. The imbalance between fluctuating market demand and the number of practicing weavers proved perennially difficult to address, compounded with currency fluctuations that exacerbated foreign market forces.

An additional concern expressed in the mid-1980s involved social changes and technological advances throughout the industry due to physical demands of the heavy Hattersley loom. By 1986 a new pioneering Bonas-Griffiths single width loom came into use as a training tool, leading to introduction of the double-width Bonas-Griffiths loom in the 1990s. This more expensive weaving machine enabled production of a lighter, less scratchy, more flexible cloth that corresponded to clothing manufacturers' new practices. Harris Tweed was poised for additional needed improvements, including conforming to European trademark law and adopting new marketing methods. Nevertheless, from its height in 1996 producing nearly seven million meters of Harris Tweed, output fell to a mere one million in 2006 when the main mill passed into English hands.

A 1989 study predicted that poor sales were an outcome of the "fashion cycle, fabric trends, [and] changing lifestyle patterns." Harris Tweed was seen as an "upmarket product, sold at low market price, without luxury product qualities" – not a winning combination. The previously predominant North American market cratered with the advent of less expensive and easy to maintain synthetic knit fabrics and the need for new designs. The essential distinction of Harris Tweed remained that the cloth was a hand-loomed craft product with a distinct geographic provenance, much as French champagne and Greek feta.

Managing Director of the Stornoway KM Harris Tweed Group Derick Murray sent shocked ripples through the industry when he put both the Stornoway and Shawbost mills, responsible for 95% of Harris Tweed output, up for sale in 2002. The move to cut losses left uncertain the future of 70 millworkers and more than 200 independent contracted weavers. A year later in 2003 the small mill in Carloway, operating since 1996 as Donald Macleod Ltd under the chairmanship of Derek Reid, was renamed Harris Tweed Textiles as a partnership with U.S. financial backing from Scottish-descended Alan Bain. Reid, former head of the Scottish Tourist Board and a former Cadbury marketing director, bought the mill in Carloway along with Bain, Scottish-American president of the American-Scottish Foundation in New York City and wealthy real estate investor.

As joint directors of Harris Tweed Textiles they brought the small venture (renamed Carloway Mill in 2005) back into production. In a refrain that would echo in the future, Director Reid requested outside financing for obtaining updated looms from mainland Scottish suppliers. At that point the Carloway mill employed only a dozen in-house workers and dealt with two dozen weavers, with extended effects estimated for an additional up to one hundred jobs. The main argument for weavers was to provide an alternative to the large Haggas-owned Mackenzie mill in Stornoway that saw its hard times as a harbinger of impending doom for the entire Harris Tweed industry. In May 2005 Harris Tweed Textiles chairman Reid became the subject of a Harris Tweed Authority legal action focused on the production site and name of its yarn. In response Reid attacked the Chair of the HTA, Ian Mackenzie – who left his post two years later to start a rival (and more successful) mill: Harris Tweed Hebrides in Shawbost.

In 2004 production jumped with the order of major U.S. global shoe manufacturer Nike for 9,500 meters of Harris Tweed to be used for 500 pairs of shoes in an effort to diversify its offerings with a new tweed-sided shoe (Figure 5.1). Fashion world attention refocused on this iconic product as a retro retooling. A Nike representative initially contacted noted Harris weaver Donald John MacKay to inquire about production of cloth for the new shoe line. Astonished by the size of the order, MacKay realized both its potential to reinvigorate Harris Tweed weaving on a world stage, and the inability of any one weaver to satisfactorily produce the amount of cloth needed. He turned to Stornoway's KM Group mill for help, at that time producing 95% of Lewis' tweed.

Figure 5.1 Lews Castle Museum display (left to right): Production Book for orders, roll of Orb mark certifications, sample color swatches, Nike Harris Tweed-covered shoe

Unfortunately, the supply of weavers capable of producing cloth at that low point in the industry was insufficient, falling from 2,000 weavers in 1970 to only 200 by 2004. Labor demands meant pulling multi-tasking crofters from seasonal farm work and causing late order fulfillment. The shoe ultimately generated insufficient sales to continue production, but MacKay and his weaver wife Maureen founded the Luskentyre Harris Tweed Company as a corporate structure for their business.

The next year in 2005 saw the closing of the KM Group Stornoway's affiliated tweed mill in the west coast town of Shawbost. The facility remained dormant for almost two more years. The Nike move signaled a step in the right direction for a successful small venture: "flexible specialization". This strategy swept the business world since the last decades of the 20th century as a significant means of transforming and preserving older manufacturing firms. It prioritized the ability to produce a basic product, whether tweed or eyeglass frames, that could be customized to customer preferences for a variety of applications. What happened next moved in the opposite and nearly deadly direction.

In December 2006 West Yorkshire textile businessman Brian Haggas purchased Stornoway's Kenneth Mackenzie mill, the tweed industry's dominant producer. He then shut down the smaller Shawbost mill, and announced his intent to dismiss single-width weavers connected with Mackenzie and the bulk of its existing staff. He further reduced to four choices the range of 8,000 patterns of vegetal-based colors reflecting the Hebridean landscape's natural setting. An additional three patterns featured a lighter weight wool in jackets. Many shared the feelings of one prominent merchant who voiced the concerns of his bespoke clients:

> ". . . the people who wear this cloth are not wearing it because they need something to keep them warm. They're wearing it because they want to feel part of this romantic history of the highlands of Scotland . . ."

Massive purchases of modern machinery flooded the factory floor with the first flush of enthusiasm by the new English owner. Mackenzie Mill tweed was to be mass-produced in large quantities designed to generate efficient industrial-size profits by primarily turning out only men's jackets in the severely restricted colors. The target market had moved from 19th century quail-hunting peers of the realm to 21st century rising middle-class Chinese flaunting their global credentials by wearing a recognizably classic British bespoke tweed business jacket.

To maximize their market, Haggas shipped his first set of 70,000 jackets to China. This move was reminiscent of the "cut and

sew kits" produced by Chinese textile fabric manufacturers that
turned out large quantities of limited choice fabric for upholstered
furniture aimed for the lower to middle end market. This type of low
cost, mass churned out manufacture would gut the U.S. furniture
industry in the last decade of the 20th century. Regeneration came
only with efficiency enhancement using lean manufacturing
techniques and most important, drawing on a custom high-end
market. Mackenzie's opposite number, small enterprises operated
by independent weavers, feared an imminent inability to obtain the
variety of yarn usually supplied by an island mill that they needed
to weave their customized, hand crafted Harris Tweed products.

Moving forward

By early 2007, grants from the Highlands and Islands
Enterprise (*Innse Gall*) government group, whose mission lay in
supporting the creation of local jobs, funded steps forward for the
struggling local industry. Brian Wilson, a former Blair cabinet
Member of Parliament, moved to his island home on Harris and
sought a savior for Shawbost's shuttered mill. He arose in the guise
of oil and gas industry entrepreneur Ian Taylor, a wealthy Scot
seeking to support a promising but struggling native enterprise.
From an unlikely but well-compensated background, oil trader
Taylor emerged to reopen the recently shuttered Shawbost mill
under the brand name of Harris Tweed Hebrides. Chief Executive
(and former head of the Harris Tweed Association) Ian Angus
Mackenzie and Sales Director Rae Mackenzie announced the newly
reopened mill would be fully functional by the first of the year with
a workforce of 25 employees. Some workers were called back from
its predecessor in the same place. Others had been furloughed from
the Stornoway facility whose sole focus on men's jackets left an
unaddressed market for Shawbost to enter. With the aid of Taylor's
substantial investment, former Harris Tweed Authority head Ian
MacKenzie (one of several well-represented Isle surnames)
assembled the local talent eager for re-engagement. In December
2007 Highlands and Islands Enterprise awarded Carloway (128,000

pounds) and Shawbost (204,000 pounds) to purchase new machinery for modernizing their operations.

Re-engagement also came with the Japanese connections of a creative director who formerly modeled in that early island textile modernizer and successful emulator of things Western. The current UK's Scotland Office Minister noted that the year of devolution saw his predecessor Brian Wilson launch a new Harris Tweed promotional brochure in Japan. Harris Tweed products also appeared on the runways of fashion showcases in Florence, Paris and London. The ensuing rocket-like takeoff is discussed in Chapter 7 – a fortuitously classic case of the right people being in the right place at the right time, with the right approach to a solvable if seemingly insurmountable problem.

The year 2008 witnessed a turbulent roller coast of events in the Harris Tweed story. The Harris Tweed Investment Fund (HTIF) invested 300,000 British pounds to train and retain weavers for the industry. An additional 82,000 pounds came to the Harris Tweed Skills Training Program drawing on funds diverted from the European Regional Development Fund. Famous Lewis songstress Alyth McCormack took Harris Tweed along in her tour wardrobe with the legendary Irish folk music group The Chieftains. Her appearance included singing a traditional waulking song while wearing a striking "thistle pink" gown. In June 2008 Yorkshire businessman Brian Haggas suspended production at the large Stornoway Kenneth Mackenzie mill, ultimately sending his 70,000 jackets for sale in China.

In March 2009 Haggas closed his mill for a year and slashed more than a dozen jobs only two years after purchasing the plant and filling it with new machinery. The same issue of the leading Stornoway newspaper that announced the devastating closing also carried articles celebrating the presentation of Harris Tweed Hebrides (Shawbost) scarves to the wives of world leaders at the 2009 G20 meeting in London. Brian Wilson, former UK Trade Minister and now chair of Harris Tweed Hebrides, defiantly and proudly declared at the time that Hebridean tweed remained "a symbol of diversity, heritage and craftsmanship."

In February 2009, the lowest production year of Harris Tweed since the mid-1930s, a Stornoway newspaper featured famous singer Alyth McCormack's light weight open weave wedding dress and long cape of Harris Tweed by noted Lewis designer Ann MacCallum, using Carloway Mill fabric in "thistle pink". The ensemble is part of a display at the Lews Castle Museum. That famous structure re-opened its doors in late 2016, following renovation of Lord Matheson's Castle. It was memorably constructed during the time of famine, exodus and struggle from which Harris Tweed first emerged as a brand in the late 19th century. History continues its ironies, and Lewis' famous fabric continues its efforts to survive along with the economy of this indomitable island outpost.

CHAPTER 6

The Dragon Leaps Overseas

"The textile industry was one of the first manufacturing industries to take on a global dimension, and it exemplifies many of the intractable issues facing today's world economy." Dicken, 1998

"Implementation of the strategy of "going out" is an important measure taken in the new stage of opening up. We should encourage and help relatively competitive enterprises . . . to invest abroad in order to increase export of goods and labor services and bring about a number of strong multinational enterprises and brand names." Chairman Jiang Zemin, 2002, 16th National Congress of the Communist Party of China (CPC)

China opened its door to foreign trade for the second time in 1978 – but this time by its own choice rather than at the barrel of a British cannon. Jardine Matheson's machinations triggering a trade war over opium in 1839, almost a century and a half before, resulted in the Treaty of Tientsin signed in 1868. Key provisions of the 19th century agreement (signed under duress in recognition of foreign military superiority) pried open several previously tightly shut Chinese ports for foreign trade. Terms of the treaty ensured the ability of foreign ships and individuals to navigate China's longest river. The Changjiang is deep enough to carry goods and influences deep into the country's interior. Like Tianjin, a port city close to Beijing, the Changjiang was formerly known in English translations as the Yangtze River; post-1949 Chinese place names were translated into the dialect spoken in the capital, known as the national or common language, or Mandarin. The treaty's ensuing turmoil, unleashed by the capsizing of traditional arrangements that kept the outside world separate from China, plunged the country into a "century of humiliation." This deeply disturbing period involved civil war, invasion in 1930 and eventual occupation by the Japanese as a precursor to World War II, and continuation of the civil war until consolidation of power by the Chinese Communist Party (CCP) in late 1949. Britain's imposition of "free trade" under duress led to a fiery future and bloody birth of a new Asian nation.

Chairman Mao Zedong's triumphal revolutionary movement launched China on a lurching path to modernization. Redistribution of wealth by land reform, agricultural collectivization, industrial socialization, and suppression of protests through the 1957 "anti-Rightist" movement followed. Stumbles along the way culminated in the following year's Great Leap Forward that launched three years of famine resulting in 12-20 million deaths. The indeterminacy of this dreadful number indicates the secrecy still surrounding these events, evident in a distinct indentation in China's population pyramid. Male and female population by age range on opposite sides of a diagram, from youngest at the base to oldest at the peak show something unusual occurred. The decade of the Great Proletarian Cultural Revolution (GPCR) from 1966-1976 plunged China into further chaos designed by its top leadership, itself in tumult under an aged but deified Mao. The death of Mao and Lin Piao, his right-hand head of the military, brought the GPCR to a close.

Pragmatic leader Deng Xiaoping's return from exile launched the second stage of China's modernization in 1978 with a new "Opening" (*gaige kaifang*) that prioritized learning from how things were done in more economically advanced countries – and then adapting and improving upon it for China's circumstances. The two-part intention of this policy lay in internal stability and strengthening through economic ascendancy via globalization. Substituting the name of the city in the slogan on a bridge in Trenton, New Jersey, the goal was "China Makes, the World Takes." What the Chinese leadership like to term their country's "peaceful rising" model of rapid export manufacturing-led growth was built on a solid base constructed under Deng's tutelage.

Hallmarks are infrastructure linking workers to labor sites and shipping facilities, a strictly enforced rule of law and predictable security of investments, cutting edge or at least appropriate level technology, and an adequate supply of motivated workers.

All elements were oriented toward producing goods for a largely export market, often in tandem with foreign companies, often in partnership in some form with Chinese firms. The average annual growth rate in Chinese exports from 1990-2004 ranged from 17% to 21%, according to calculations of the United Nations Conference on Trade and Development. All such calculations involve some informed speculation, since the official goal was a 7% growth rate of the economy to dampen concerns over possible inflation and over-heating.

Launching Chinese Outward Foreign Direct Investment

Studies of Chinese Outward Foreign Direct Investment (COFDI) generally fall into two camps: 1) COFDI as an outcome of the national level central government's political-economic strategy, or 2) a business strategy for achieving firm goals. Chief among the latter are 1) gaining market access for product sales, 2) obtaining new talent and technology, 3) leveraging the home market by introducing it to newly accessible products, 4) utilizing a cost advantage with less expensive land, labor or capital, and/or 5) taking advantage of low credit costs. Studies consistently note that the Chinese government encourages COFDI as a means of acquiring advanced technology, notable recognized brands, and resources not in sufficient domestic supply.

The year 2015 notched a high mark for COFDI, with an estimated US$1 trillion in completed deals. Transaction value hit $61 billion, similar to that in 2013, but fell from the 2013 peak of 10% of global mergers and acquisitions (M&A). Retail remained a small but increasing (from negligible pre-2014) sector of completed outbound COFDI in the decade 2005-15. By the year 2005 textile manufacturing employed the largest number of workers (8,000) of any industry in China, fueling large export volume and earnings.

Aside from competitive price advantage, this segment became known for 24-hour shift work, speedy response to market demand, and helpful suggestions for improvements in process. In general, Chinese investments over time trended away from resource sector acquisitions to feature a broader array of higher-level sectors. Movement was away from production of basic commodities such as textiles, toward more elite skill level production and advanced economy targets such as technology and financial services.

Interest in Europe as a location for Chinese investments soared since the 2008 recession presented low cost acquisition opportunities. Chinese government funding furnished the means and encouragement for companies to act. Renewed U.S. security concerns stalled several COFDI bids to purchase companies or controlling stock in firms considered of strategic interest in the target country. European nations, on the other hand, put out a welcome mat for outside funds in hopes of alleviating their own financial troubles. Acquisition of advanced technology, real estate, and well-recognized name brands present top targets for investment in advanced economies, rather than the strategic natural resources that characterize developing world acquisitions by China. Harris Tweed became attractive when fashionable actors and sports figures began to wear it. The iconic fabric then caught the attention of China's newly prosperous and globe-trotting, trend-conscious upper class. Private companies located on China's booming east coast provinces led the way, such as textile giant Shandong Ruyi. Shandong Province was the birthplace of the sage Confucius, and the German-Japanese colonial possession that sparked the May 4th Movement precursor to the Chinese communist revolution.

Out of the 30 billion euros invested in Europe by the end of 2013, the UK claimed a 12,212 million euro share nearly double that of runner-up Germany since the year 2000. Aside from the top target location of London, Scotland attracted the most UK investments from China, particularly in manufacturing such as the joint venture with Carloway Mill. Scotland remained the second largest target of FDI in 2017, with 14% of its exports going to China – the highest level on record. By mid-2017 China chalked up 3.6% of UK exports, and 7% of its imports. The 82 Scottish COFDI projects chalked up in 2013 set a record since 1997, even eclipsing those purchased in 2014. Europe continued as the top draw for COFDI in 2014 and 2017, eclipsing the U.S. largely due to the latter's national security concerns that blocked several proposed acquisitions. Over the decade from 2005-2015 as a whole, the U.S. led as a COFDI destination with a total of US$ 93.3 billion investments, followed by Australia with 76.5 billion (including resource purchases such as wool for cotton in 2015), Canada (42.9), Brazil (34.3), Nigeria (32.2, largely for fossil fuel), Indonesia (31.6), Russia (30.2) and the UK in eighth place (29.2).

The British Embassy featured Harris Tweed and gin at a June 2018 exhibition touting goods for export to Asia. Japan was the #19 export destination for particularly Scottish goods. Lorna Macauley, chief executive of the Harris Tweed Authority, noted at the time that "Japan continues to be a vitally important premium export market for Harris Tweed. Japanese consumers understand and appreciate color, texture and hand-craftsmanship so evident in Harris Tweed cloth."

The developed countries of Western Europe serve primarily as a target for manufacturing mergers and acquisitions due to their strength in advanced manufacturing with a more extensive use of machinery, robotics, and higher skilled rather than routine labor employees. Total COFDI investments in Europe over the decade were, in order, agriculture and food, energy, real estate (with London a popular target for international OFDI in general), automotive, and finance/ business services. Developing countries were targeted basically for resource access such as fossil fuel surpluses, while developed countries were seen as potentially supplying advanced information and practices that China needed to learn. Adaptation of cutting-edge technology from overseas targeted development of "Made in China "products for export to these same developed world markets in the future, with higher value-added profit margins.

Middle Eastern and Central Asian "One Belt, One Road" (OBOR) countries attracted relatively less Chinese economic interest, despite highlighted government policies, than commercial possibilities in EU countries. The latest development push to spread China's outside influence involves construction of goods-moving infrastructure from rails and roads to sea and air ports. Goals include creating new economic partners in less-developed countries who will benefit from location on a China-centered trade route running from China to every corner of the world.

Investing in the UK

Purchase of UK commercial concerns and properties seem attractive due to the possibilities of an investment-infused turn-around from introduction of more advanced technology. COFDI tends to use local high skill workers and management techniques rather than the complete overhaul experienced in previous Japanese corporate take-overs. Investment positions vary from outright purchases to equity or contractual joint ventures, reflecting, respectively, the amount of money invested or the amount of control negotiated. The latter could reflect the value placed on a partner's expertise rather than its relative sunk capital in the company. Residential property purchases constitute another star attraction for COFDI and a major magnet for financial activities in the UK.

Within Europe in 2013-15 the United Kingdom led in both the number of FDI projects and FDI-linked job creation. In 2013 China's OFDI increased by 23% from the previous year, and an average of 40% in the previous decade. With an investment of US$ 18 billion in 2014, Chinese companies were the fifth largest FDI investors in Europe. This represented a doubling of their previous year's investment and ahead of the former Asian economic power of Japan, a signifier of the Chinese economy surpassing that island nation for the first time. A survey of companies with current foreign direct investment portfolios evaluated their experiences with the top three destinations for investments; Western Europe led the list in both 2014 and 2015 (see Table 6.1).

Table 6.1 Global Business Survey of Most Attractive Region to Establish Operations

	2014	2015
Western Europe	45%	50%
U.S.	31%	39%
China	44%	38%

Source: Ernst & Young European Investment Monitor 2015

By 2017 China was the fifth highest source of FDI to Scotland. This continued a three-year surge in foreign investments to Scotland.

A national economic security question frequently raised in the popular media concerns the amount of Chinese government involvement in the acquiring company. The case of Shandong Ruyi involved a large and unusually profitable state-owned enterprise (SOE). Less government-affiliated COFDI firms are often left to their own devices, aside from some favorable initial loans available from Chinese sources. These firms appear quite obedient to local laws and regulations, and the Chinese government would not want negative publicity on this issue. Some questions remain regarding the use of local labor and transfer of technological "know-how" from China to the country where projects are being constructed. These issues seem to be more sensitive in the U.S. than in Europe, which is hungrier for foreign investment. Non-SOEs investing abroad rose, although SOEs by their very nature are individually much larger and have far more to invest than true private ventures. Chinese investments in the UK traded positions with those from the U.S. in the post-recession 2011-2014 period, indicating a new foreign investment source on the horizon (Table 6.2).

Table 6.2   UK Earning from FDI in Textiles and Wool

Source	2011	2012	2013	2014
EU	196	420	212	296
USA	333	303	97	87

Source: British Wool Marketing Board; Highlands & Islands Enterprise

Overall COFDI in the UK grew annually by 85% since the 2008 downturn. From nearly negligible prior to 2008, investment in 2009 reached US$ 3 billion. It more than tripled the following year and the year after, for a total post-2008 investment of US$ 455 billion flowing to Europe from China. The global recession of 2008 whetted Chinese appetites for investment in new, diverse sectors that seemed to hold promise for future expansion. Britain soared to be the top market for COFDI in 2015 with US$ 5.1 billion in capital investments. Within the EU, major sectors for COFDI investment from 2000-2014 denominated in USD were in energy (417 billion), automotive (7.7 billion), agriculture (6.9 billion), real estate (6.4 billion), industrial equipment (5.3 billion) and information and communications technology (3.5 billion).

This trajectory reflected opportunities the Chinese government saw to sustain their economy by funding bargain purchases during a global downturn, raising fears of European desperation leading to a "fire sale" of underpriced companies. Interests in areas such as energy shifted over this period reflecting an over-abundance relative to demand. Commercial real estate picked up sharply as an investment interest in 2013 and 2014, driven by an increasing outflow of Chinese students, emigrants and tourists venturing abroad who also found desirable consumer products to both purchase and invest in for future gain. Areas of European strengths such as widely recognized brand names (goods and companies) and technology (established and innovative) also draw Chinese investment interest as high visibility prestigious and promising targets for acquisition or position taking. A focus on mergers and acquisitions and investment in established businesses dominated. They were likely to continue as favored targets attracting suitors by the value of potential investment returns. Risks of debuting a new firm as a "greenfield" venture overseas were understandably seen as too precarious, rather than placing a joint venture bet on a known foreign firm or extending a strong, proven domestic firm with tested competitive attributes.

Targeted COFDI sectors varied by country, logically reflecting a particular country's relative strength and indicating some research on the part of investors: food sectors in France, real estate in the UK, machinery in Germany, R&D in Nordic countries, food and agriculture in the Netherlands, an energy company in Italy, insurance firms in Portugal. Taking an interest in and purchasing positions in logistics links to handle shipment of these products of interest (see Table 6.3) raised skill levels. A more fully integrated vertical production chain, less vulnerable to outside interference, was developing. Chinese shipping firms now frequently carry trade commodities directly to their Asian destinations.

Table 6.3 Top European Countries for COFDI (US$ billion)

Country	2014	Since 2000	2018 (1st half)
Sweden			3.6
U.K.	5.1	16	1.6
Germany	1.6	8.4	1.5
France		8	1.4
Portugal	2.0	6.7	
Italy	3.5	5.6	
Netherlands	2.3	4	

Source: Baker & McKenzie, 2015; Bloomburg 2018

Investing abroad serves the additional function of diversifying China's large foreign asset reserves accumulated from its decades-long role as a "global factory" churning out exports unleashed by its transition to the manufacturing stage of development takeoff. Sovereign wealth funds target regulated and open opportunities in areas such as real estate and infrastructure – the former popular in both the US and UK, the latter less so in the US. Moving up the value chain by accessing production and services-aligned knowledge continues to be a priority for next-stage Chinese development. The opacity of Chinese firms feeds concerns by foreign companies, countries and investors familiar with more extensive transparency requirements.

Proposals for countering Chinese transactional opacity include calls for a more united European front to monitor and mitigate security vulnerabilities that are seen as legitimate and as yet unaddressed. This issue could be ironed out over time as Chinese firm increasingly utilize UK business services such as lawyers, accountants, and other business middlemen who seek to ease their market entry and promote local standard operating procedures. The growth of nascent Chinese investment pools of various amounts correspondingly increased diversity in the size of investment targets. These include small and medium ventures of part ownership, rather than large full scale purchases that predominated in the past, usually by SOEs with government deep pockets. This type of activity led to Ruyi's contribution to Carloway Mill's tweed enterprise at a more limited scale than some of its other ventures.

The monetary amount of COFDI in general, and in the United Kingdom and Scotland in particular, is relatively small. This is also the case compared to the amount of foreign investment pouring into China from the UK and the amount of FDI to other countries from non-Chinese sources. In the case of the Chinese joint venture with the Harris Tweed mill, advantage calculations stemmed from obtaining a well-known prestigious brand name that was seen to reflect well on the Chinese company. It also enabled taking advantage of an opportunity to invest in a small, relatively affordable mill with a rapidly increasing sales volume but needing capital input to improve the technology in a field that the purchasing company was quite familiar with: textiles.

Shandong Ruyi Science and Technology Group

Currently a conglomerate involved in a variety of ventures globally, Shandong Ruyi (SR) began on December 28, 1993 under its current chairman: Shandong native Qiu Yafu. As a corporate entity it grew from the Jining Wool Textile Factory originally established in 1972 during the Cultural Revolution. Similar to India's Reliant Industry, now one of the largest companies in India and one of many foreign joint venture partners with Ruyi, the textile industry was its initial business base. Since the Industrial Revolution in the mid-1800s textiles has been one of the first products to substitute machines for human labor. The numerous

low skill jobs created in the process sped the transition off the
fields and into Industrial production, at a basic level. In 1996
Shandong Ruyi became a "state individual proprietorship".

By 2001 Ruyi's activities were large enough to justify its
own "Ruyi Hi-tech Industry Park in Jining Hi-tech Development
Zone" specializing in textile production and research. Four years
later the company expanded to the west China city of Chongqing.
There it established a large spinning factory, following central
government incentives to "Develop the West" region of China.
Ruyi company shares debuted with an IPO (initial public offering
of stock) in 2007 on the Shenzhen stock exchange, marking their
"coming out" on the domestic investment stage. In 2010 Rui
purchased the largest share of stock in a large Japanese clothes
manufacturer. By 2013 the highly automated production process
utilized 3,000 weaving machines of various types from the four
developed countries noted above, setting 330,000 spindles
whirring. Global sales that year hit USD$5 billion, keeping more
than 40,000 employees busy worldwide.

The Shandong Jining Ruyi Woolen Textile Co. Ltd., a
specialized division of the company, focuses on producing and
marketing worsted woolen textiles at more than 20 plants. Products
include suits, fashions for the luxury and leisure/Lycra market,
scarves, "intelligent technology" and "ecologic" wool lines. After
establishing a dominant position in the Chinese textile industry and
domestic market, the Ruyi Group went global with a targeted
investment strategy. Their market penetration reaches into over 50
countries, largely in Asia, Europe and North America. A timeline
of highlighted acquisitions includes the following milestones,
providing context for their Harris Tweed mill interest.

Year
2011   Japanese trading conglomerate Itochu with Asian textile
interest (Chester Barrie, Paul Smith) purchases a 30% share in SR.
A giant trading company, the Itochu Corporation ranks just below
Mitsubishi in size. Its base lies with its textile division, particularly
due to links with China since 1972. Its fortunes also rose in tandem

with those of India's Reliance Industries which took off in the 1970s by supplying synthetic polyester yarn to that rapidly developing venture. Itochu's investment became the largest investment by a Japanese trading company in India's economy at that point. Its investment in 2015 in CITIC Group, a Chinese SOE, was the largest investment in China by a Japanese trading company. Itochu's 2011 "equity method associated company" investment in Rui, "founded as a state-owned worsted woolen textile factory", is seen as facilitating access to China's domestic textile market and its global chain of business interests in an integrated value chain.

2012   Harris Tweed sales hit highest point in 20 years.

2013   March: Joint venture agreement with Carloway Mill, smallest and financially most fragile of three HT mills. Some concerns expressed that this might be preliminary to a merger and acquisition (M&A) move, which proved unfounded. Also purchases Australian fine cotton "Cubbie" firm to obtain quality raw material.
        December: announces intent to acquire a majority (52%) stake in Pakistan's Masood Textile Mills; attempt later cancelled. Announces interest in Pakistan Cotton Ginners Association to improve cotton and yarn export;

2014   January: Ruyi purchases a majority partnership with the German Peine Group, makers of men's high fashion clothing. Introduces two brands to the Asia market. Peine was experiencing financial difficulties, so happy for SR to supply backing.
        February: Ruyi acquires an 80% stake in Yorkshire textile mill "Taylor and Lodge" luxury worsted wool; balance held by British "Bulmer & Lumb Group";
        April: Invests in a Pakistani Apparel Park;
        September: Minority share in British "TM Lewin";
        December: Textile joint venture (49/51) with Reliance International, India's most profitable private company, as an entry

into the South Asian market with SR's family of brands from England, China, Italy and Harris Tweed; Company sales overall drop by 1.7% by the end of 2014 from a high point in 2013. Woolen textile sales take a sharper dive with a 9% sales decrease. The unstable economy of Asia in general – and Japan in particular, which purchased 40% of Hebridean cloth output in 2013 – impacted downward sales of luxury fashion wear.

2015   Retrenchment follows global over-expansion in 2013, including TM Lewin management's buy back of 20% of the company's shares thanks to investment from a subsidiary (Sankaty) U.S. venture capital turn-around specialists Bain Capital (later connected to HT). The CEO reportedly held 30%, with the remaining half owned by the management team. A new twist in Ruyi's COFDI chapter begins to unfold.

With assets in 2015 of US$375 million and around 20,000 Chinese employees in several branch locations, Shandong Ruyi (SR) ranks as one of the top ten textile companies in China and one of the top 100 businesses in Shandong Province. Textile related activities include woolen textiles, rabbit hair spinning, spandex fiber, garments, cotton textiles and denim, printing and dyeing, knitting jeans and real estate. Certifications for excellence in manufacturing quality include ISO9001 and ISO14001. Machinery for their factories originates in Germany, Switzerland, Italy and Japan. This indicates their intention to use high quality equipment. The printing and dyeing division turns out "African figured cloth" for that continent's mass market, as well as upscale products for export to the more developed world.

2016   February: winning bid for French KKR & Co. SMCP.
March: purchase of French fashion group SMCP, with its three popular clothing brands; deal value 1.3 billion euros. SJR goes on a buying spree, adding to its portfolio a Hond Kong menswear group and British luxury clothing manufacturer.

2017   Purchase of a major stock position in a luxury Swiss brand, and in the running to buy a British fashion company. By the end of 2017, Shandong Ruyi was China's largest textile manufacturer, dominant in the clothing supply chain, and a highly profitable luxury fashion group.

The Chinese economic "dragon" had indeed extended its reach overseas and proved in the case of the Jilin Ruyi textile firm to be the sea-leaping "turtle" envisioned in the Chinese leadership's exhortation for modernization by merger and acquisition. But rapid ingestion can easily lead to indigestion, posting a potential problem for this conglomerate with a rapidly expanding waistline. Shandong Ruyi discovered that several of its troubled firm purchases were not susceptible to easy or rapid turnarounds. Much remained to be learned about the workings of capitalism. Some lessons proved more painful than others. Global economic threats came in the form of events difficult to foresee, such as the 2008 recession. This threatened to swamp many boats, particularly those venturing far from accustomed ports such as overseas foreign direct investments. Issues involving relatively tiny Carloway Mill were ignored, while larger company concerns were tackled. This inevitably came back to trouble its foreign junior partner. What to do with a Scottish textile mill proud of its 19th century equipment and cottage weavers, when China proudly boasted of its huge factories with cutting edge European machines spinning world record amounts of thread? Chinese management paid the mill a visit, and were not pleased with what they saw on this remote Hebridean textile factory. An inspector shook his head while closely looking at the date of a historic late 19th century machine. Scots are pleased at the durability of such an investment, which Carloway has featured on its webpage.

CHAPTER 7

Tides in Global Trade: Recession Rebound

"I think it's so important that we, as the custodians of the orb, make sure it's not going to suffer from the slumps that it has in the past." Kathy Macaskill, Carloway Mill 2011

"Haggas destroyed the mill [Stornoway] but saved the industry [by giving rise to Shawbost]." Weaver, 2016

"Shandong Ruyi China textile maker ready for 'new normal' . . . From now on, China's economy will be more stable and based on quality." Beijing, March 2015

Harris Tweed production dipped below 1 million meters annually in 1998, the first time since its leap above that line in 1935. The year following the onset of the 2008 crash and recession set a new low point, marking a remarkable decade of mills closing, reconfiguring, being purchased and reopening, as narrated in Chapter 5. The Tweed industry's steady bounce back since then reaped seeds sown in the lean decade. The turn-around lesson differs for each of the three functioning Harris Tweed mills. The variety of outcomes signals the importance of and opportunities inherent in management decisions. They also provide lessons concerning the sustainability of a model made by a modernizing product tightly bound to an identified key distinction such as its historic provenance of place and quality.

General rejoicing greeted the announcement in March 2013 that Chinese textile giant Shandong Jilin Ruyi had invested as a joint venture partner in the Carloway Mill. The year 2012 banner production of more than one million meters attracted Ruyi's attention, as outlined in the previous chapter. The mill's manager Anne Mackenzie noted that past funding came largely from mill owners (such as her husband), and expressed relief at receiving the joint venture's infusion of funds. Access to the booming Chinese market, driven by a new middle and upper class patronizing new shopping malls, in addition to Ruyi's contacts in 50 other countries, provided hope for a profitable future.

Anticipated use of the new funds included plans to purchase new machinery and construct new space to house it, while waiting for Chinese market orders to pour in. An oft-cited issue in the textile industry, common to other retail concerns, lies in the need to initially invest in production infrastructure prior to realizing profits. This requires investors to possess "patient capital" with deep pockets. Aspiring capitalists must be capable of investing a significant sum and withstanding a long wait for returns on the investment. Such individuals and companies are few, especially for a small, remote island enterprise whose management they do not control.

Spring Weather

Rays of hope appeared to shine over a near horizon, as detailed in the previous chapter. In late October 2015 Britain's Prime Minister Cameron and China's President Xi Jinping gathered congenially in London to proclaim a "strategic partnership for the 21st century". Their confidence included predictions of a smooth ride ahead for China's "one belt, one road" policy promoting trade ties linking Asia and Europe as in the good old Silk Road days when (almost) all roads led to Rome. The ambitious global infrastructure project's name invoked empire-era days when the Roman market clamored for China's iconic silk textile with a highly protected secret production process. China again sought to turn its manufacturing tide to exports, bringing in foreign currency to relieve its over-production/ under-consumption problems and increase employment of Chinese labor. China's projected annual tourist outflow of 100 million people venturing abroad contributed 500 million pounds to the British economy. This outflow was largely thanks to China's new middle class, built by a successful manufacturing and real estate-based economy raising millions of people from agricultural to low-paid manufacturing work, spreading capital to an unprecedented proportion of China's economy.

Chinese planners promised to keep Britain in the monetary circulation loop, via its brand name products and prestigious historical destinations from castles to cashmere, the Tower to tweed. British tourism officials estimated that for every 22 Chinese tourists, spending an average of just under 3,000 pounds each, one UK job appeared to address the demand for goods and services. Chinese acquisitions in the European hospitality industry as of mid-2016 included high to mid-end hotels with their restaurant and conference facilities, real estate, retail and recreational outlets such as cinemas. Focus on this sector indicated a developing strategy of keeping more Chinese money spent abroad within the Chinese corporate circuit. Travelers in a foreign country, especially those less experienced in being abroad, prefer to stay in places that literally and figuratively speak their language.

The mutual pay off for China and the UK was both obvious and desirable, though most of the economic largess for the UK ended up in London. Excited estimates in mid-2015 forecast $20 trillion in Chinese Outward Foreign Direct Investment (COFDI) by 2020, largely flowing to Europe. A frequently employed cautionary phrase in statistical forecasts is *ceteris parebus* – roughly translatable as "all things remaining equal", meaning holding all but one factor constant. This tends to work much better in statistics than in the more complex interactions of reality. Zooming from zero COFDI in the European Union (EU) sphere at the turn of the 21st century to 14 billion euros by 2014 does not imply a constantly increasing trajectory, as the history of economic investments amply illustrates. It does however indicate a new direction for developing countries trading on a combination of competitive labor and material cost and skill underwritten by government policy seeking advancement to the next, higher level.

As the UK's sixth largest export market and consumer of 3.6% of Britain's goods and services, China was a player but did not yet loom large in the global trade game. More ominously, given the unlucky characteristics of the numbers four and 10 for the Chinese (with only a tonal distinction separating them from the word for "deceased"), growth in their economy was slowing to a rate of 4% and unemployment ranged from 4-10% in the final quarter of 2015. Typically for the Outer Hebrides, sunny economic weather was also proving fleeting, with highly changeable conditions reverting to the more common gray and uncertain outlook. Storms moving in over Asia's strongest economy, however, might portend positive results for Carloway, the smallest and most fragile textile mill according to several economic forecasts.

Clouds Part and Reappear

A global economic slowdown in late 2014 triggered concerns regarding overproduction and wage escalation, leading the National People's Congress to reduce China's expected annual growth rate. Ruyi's chairman responded by predicting that his company's future growth would come from "automation and computerization". This was not a good sign for a small, custom, labor-intensive Harris Tweed operation. Particularly when a rise in resource costs in materials such as wool were specifically cited – an assumed reason for Ruyi's acquisitions in an Australian sheep farm. Favorable relative labor costs in less developed textile producing countries such as India, Pakistan and Bangladesh also contrasted unfavorably with wage increases for weavers in Scotland. The goal of consolidating the production chain within China included establishing well-recognized brands. This differs from acquiring an allied share of foreign brands with no domestic links other than access to China's vast market. Similarities with Japanese corporate culture and a desire to learn from Japanese advanced management methods, two aspects of Ruyi's interests with parent company Itochu, did not apply in the case of Harris Tweed. Local Lewis management was much more resistant to change both in equipment and management practices, preferring those more in line with local customary practices.

The British textile trade publication "Drapers News" in mid-February 2016 headlined an enticing set of facts in bright red and gold. With a population of 1.4 billion representing 19% of the world's total, a 6.9% rate of economic growth in 2015 (remarkably close to the 7% projected target), and a forecast 6% drop in 2016 of the value of the *yuan* currency, China saw a rise of 33.3% in online retail sales in 2015. Sales of garments, footwear, hats and knitwear represented 9.8%. The cautionary headline read: "Into the dragon's den of Chinese retail". Opportunities of a large potential market beckoned, but looking into the headwinds of a possibly stalling – or segmenting – economy, was the underlying message. The first quarter of 2016 saw China posting its highest recorded value of mergers and acquisitions (US$101 billion), more than in the entire year of 2015 (US$109 billion). Chinese OFDI in Europe (US$23 billion) significantly surpassed its flow to the US in 2015 (US$17 billion), reflecting easier (less politically sensitive) access to the market in general and the nature of its acquisition targets in particular. Europe remained hungry for outside investment to shore up its financial recovery, and was less sensitive to the relatively high presence (70%) of State Owned Enterprises (SOEs) among Chinese companies. These are capable of bankrolling more expensive ventures overseas, but also contain the liabilities of connection to the central Chinese government and related State interests.

China's financial ill winds could ultimately blow in Lewis' favor, however. Capital seeks a safe haven in stormy weather, and significant amounts of Chinese capital fled the country's uncertainties to more secure investments overseas - from real estate to relatives, stock markets to corporate acquisitions and positions. Since mid-2014, an estimated more than US$1 trillion flowed out of China. The central government dipped into its bountiful foreign currency reserves in an attempt to staunch the flow, in addition to intervening in an increasingly panicked domestic stock market. Two of the four major means of moving money out of China involved individuals conveying up to $50,000 for friends or family to hold for them overseas or buying life insurance policies with Chinese currency but at dollar value. The lax credit checks authorized by Chinese card issuing authorities such as banks unused to business beyond the usual accounts secured by deposits had caused concern for a number of years. Cardholders now saw these as an opportunity to translate credit limits to push purchase limits and move money out of Chinese funders and into foreign commodities or accounts through expenditures.

More significant steps involved corporations that could acquire businesses valued up to one billion USD or "under invoicing" exports. This term referred to a shady practice of declaring goods exported at less than their full value and realizing the difference by the buyer depositing the remainder in an overseas bank. The former step taking the accustomed M&A route could simply accelerate a movement already underway and encouraged by governments such as the UK, which inked a highly anticipated accord between the countries in late 2015. The COFDI investment step also augured hope for companies like Carloway representing an established firm with a prestigious brand, but a bit wobbly on the business side. Headwinds driving an unseemly flow of funds in different directions shook the control-inclined Chinese authorities to take steps restricting the geysering of currency. It remained to be seen how effective these might prove. A society that worked ways around the Internet's "Great Firewall" of information access suppression might also experience difficulties steering the unfamiliar ship of global capitalism.

More studies of the political as well as economic effects of Chinese Outward Foreign Direct Investment could provide useful insights regarding COFDI in various sectors and countries. These should also be sensitive to time, place, and product contexts in addition to COFDI effects in themselves. This study of Chinese investment in a small textile mill on a remote, somewhat isolated Scottish island, involving a globally familiar, historically place-resonant name brand, provides insights into the trans-national operations of conglomerates in one specific product area.

Straws in the Wind

The Japanese luxury level supplies the largest market representing 60-90% for Harris Tweed, followed by Germany and North America. Harris Tweed proclaimed its re-entry to the fashion world on several fronts during the first decade and a half of the 21st century. On the publicity side, "Tweed Runs" became a global affair with tweed-clad participants engaging in foot races in trendy cities from Toronto to Tokyo, Glasgow to San Francisco. Scotland heralded its own favorite fabric with Harris Tweed picked as Textile Brand of the Year in 2009. The only five-star hotel in Glasgow, recently named a top European Cultural City, adorned its interiors with proudly Scottish Harris Tweed. Eight years after Nike failed to secure enough material to market its tweed-clad sneakers, several fashion houses successfully used Harris Tweed in their boot and footwear collections for both genders (Figure 7.1).

Figure 7.1 Fashion re-envisioned for women and men

The most potential shift for sustaining the Harris Tweed industry lies in its flexible adoption in a variety of cloth products in addition to clothing. These include children's toys, women's purses and jewelry, computer cases, shawls, and essentially anything else textile: the flexible specialization response to an increasingly global market. Little cooperation appears among the mills, however, regarding steps to sustain the industry as a whole rather than increase the profits of their own specialized segments.

Stornoway Reconfigures

At the depths of the 2008 global economic downturn, the Haggas mill announced its closure for a year beginning in early March of 2009. A vast inventory of shiny new modern machinery stood idle while the new management that had ambitiously ordered them decided how to proceed. Sensing a major mistake and an opportunity ebbing, the long-lived (since 1906) Stornoway tweed plant now operating as Harris Tweed Kenneth Mackenzie wisely expanded the range of their output. After severely curtailing offerings to only four options after purchasing the former KM Group facilities in late 2006, Mackenzie now offers 11 choices for its traditional men's jackets, including both heavier and lighter weight fabrics. Weavers purportedly like the ability of the mill's modern machinery to spray on a finish smoothing the yarn, making it easier to handle. The large number of batches in fewer varieties also reduces the time needed to tie on the yarn for a continuous roll. Employment remains severely reduced from earlier levels, and the once leading firm now represents around 5% of the total Harris Tweed market, similar to the share of much smaller Carloway Mill.

Carloway Seeks Survival

New and surprising clouds darkened the horizon of a Harris Tweed producer shortly after the declaration of Highlands and Islands Enterprise-funded expansion at the rival Harris Tweed

Hebrides (HTH) mill. The Carloway mill perches on a hillside overlooking sheep pastures in the village of Garenin, with HTH further south in the village of Shawbost. Carloway's imagery evokes a place where "heritage, language, culture and tradition meet to make beautiful bespoke Harris Tweed." In mid-January 2016 the management of Carloway Mill declared that they were running up unsupportable deficits, and contemplating entering "voluntary administration", a form of bankruptcy proceedings initiated by the company rather than creditors.

At the time The Carloway Mill accounted for approximately 6% (1.7 million meters) of Harris Tweed's total production output. By early 2016 Carloway Mill carried 27 people on its payroll, more than twice the number involved since its purchase a decade earlier, and supplied thirty weavers with yarn. This represented a healthy increase of half a dozen who were independently supplied by mills with which they were affiliated by long-term relationships. Weavers utilized either machine warped beams for Griffiths looms or the traditional hand warped yarn beamed for the older single-width Hattersley looms. Marked company vans picked up the tweed from weaver's homes and delivered it back for human inspection followed by machined washing, stretching, drying, cropping, and finally inspection by a visiting Harris Tweed Authority stamp wielder to authenticate. Around 380 inhabitants of the designated Outer Hebrides islands reportedly sustain – and are sustained by – the mandated local tweed industry as a whole. While Carloway Mill offers an average of 30 rolls of tweed for weekly HTA inspection and certification, the Shawbost mill supplies ten times that amount.

Derek Reid, one of the triumvirate of Carloway's directors at the time, claimed that a 30% rise in costs for wool (from 106 to 128 British pounds), wages for weavers (from 130 to 175 British pounds) and stamped certification by the HTA (from 8 to 26 British pounds) combined with a 10% fall in profits from the sale of Harris Tweed led to an insurmountable debt scenario. In response he proposed an additional subsidy of 200,000 British pounds from the Highlands and Islands Enterprise association. The rival tweed mill in Shawbost received a much-heralded 204,000 British pounds in the preceding month of December. Reid's intent in part was to purchase new carding machines to meet more orders, which would in turn incur more debt. The alternative lay in a threatened sale of Carloway Mill. But under that scenario, who would buy?

The three-man team administering Carloway Mill, including the two original turn-around team investors plus the husband of the Mill's Manager MacKenzie, announced an investment of their own capital in the company so that outstanding orders through April could be fulfilled. The wait for a new buyer continued, but with brighter prospects thanks to a cleaner balance sheet following the latest capital infusion. Their argument for renewed outside funding rested on the reported increase in costs of wool and weavers which the profit from even a full bookings book could not bridge. Activity at the two other Harris Tweed mills continued unabated, however, with record orders accumulating. Weavers were also reportedly unhappy with Carloway's contention that a rise in wages negotiated by the Weaver's Association helped push the mill to the brink of insolvency. Carloway's additional roles as supplier of yarn and product transit for the remaining single-width weavers and its place on the tourist trail on the middle west coast were cited as reasons to sustain the mill's existence. Such arguments were also employed to hopefully attract another investor such as the "off island" party with whom they'd reportedly been in conversation.

In mid-March 2016 one of Carloway's owners called for a one-million-pound infusion of new outside investment to fund an anticipated doubling of demand in the Asian market, predicted by their current Chinese investor Shandong Ruyi (SJR). A group from SJR arrived at Carloway a month later, shaking heads at historic machinery from the late 19th century (Figure 7.2). Up to that point, in typical COFDI fashion, the Chinese investors appeared to have little interaction with their partial acquisition. Problems in other of their many far-flung investments drew their attention first, before focus fell on the small, remote Scottish textile mill. In return for a 25% share in the mill (rather than the 51% they originally wanted and usually obtained from their numerous investments in other companies), the Chinese team proposed putting in modern machinery. This was the obvious way to generate larger volume and therefore larger profits similar to those in their huge Chinese plants. Carloway owners proclaimed the "traditional craft machinery" was used to make custom products that reflected "authenticity, sustainability, ethical . . . manufacturing." A new slogan being mooted about was "Crafted from yesterday, for tomorrow". Several textile buyers implicated the shortage of modern machinery, however, in slow order fulfillment that discouraged further business with this charming little mill.

Figure 7.2 Historic Carloway Mill heritage machinery

A Carloway Mill officer commented that despite Ruyi's wall of Harris Tweed swatches prominently on display in their Shandong headquarters, the Chinese conglomerate took little action to support and sell tweed produced by their 2003 corporate investment. More was expected through utilizing SJR's global network of over fifty sales representatives. Opportunistic purchases of other companies in the year that they acquired Carloway led to larger unanticipated problems from a deep debt position that distracted them from

attending to their tweed mill's challenges. A case of corporate
indigestion, miscommunication and missed opportunities prevailed.

Shawbost Shows a Way

Eager and open to address a new market, Shawbost's Harris
Tweed Hebrides (HTH) mill pioneered a "Smart Textile" for
premier Scotch brand Johnnie Walker in 2014. Micro-encapsulating
scent chips in a custom blended tartan weave was specifically
designed to complement the shades of whiskey. Advertising
included a place-evocative pose of HTH model, Creative Director
and brand promoter Mark Hogarth, atop a pile of peat on the Barvas
moor, sipping a wee dram of the golden liquid while draped in the
bespoke scented tweed. Getting into the act of place-linked product
promotion, another weaver designed a "Callanish Tartan"
accompanied by a "Callanish Whiskey" purportedly distilled by
moonlight next to the famed ring of megaliths in the nearby town of
Callanish (now using the more Gaelic spelling "Calanais").

In addition to partnering with Johnnie Walker, HTH fabrics
have been designed for and featured in creations by fashion houses
Prada, Ralph Lauren (U.S.), Lagerfeld (German), Victoria
Westwood (British), Kenzo and Miyake (Japan), Chanel and
Comme de Garcons (French). Currently representing 90% of the
Harris Tweed produced and sold, HTH hit the million meter mark
in 2012, followed by an additional .2 million meters the next year,
and a continuing upward demand curve. Approximately one-third of
the mill's output goes to the domestic UK market, another third to
Japan, and the remaining third elsewhere, particularly to North
America and Asian countries such as Korea. Top grade cheviot wool
is supplied from a variety of principally off-island sources. Design
work is done on the premises as well as by custom order from
outside designers who work through Asian buyers as middlemen for
other clients. Relatively recent applications of Harris Tweed for use
on upholstered furniture and accessories supplies steady orders,
reducing the seasonality of clothing that tends toward cooler
weather wear.

Based on his six-month modeling sojourn in Japan, HTH Creative Director Mark Hogarth's recipe for global success includes "creating a perfectly made textile that will last forever . . . [and is considered a] luxury because of the process it represents." This approach fits with the model Toyota production system emulated in a wide variety of products for its emphasis on zero defect manufacturing, and *kaizen* continuous improvement and checking for quality. Quality is assumed, and reflected in price. He further asserts, based on his experience modeling there, that the Japanese are fascinated by this Western fashion because it makes Hollywood glamour from the 1960s and '70s accessible to a broader market. A conscious attempt is made to twist around the product image. Examples include a slender purple corset with Agatha Christie's Miss Jane Marple image, along with purple Converse sneakers made in Japan. Outfits from the "Skyfall" James Bond movie set in Scotland play on images of tweed clothes worn by Dr. Who and actors in the movie "Australia" set in the 1940s.

Activities such as "craft, design, bold brand story, developing a brand" are credited for Shawbost mill's success along with promotional activities such as a Tokyo Harris Tweed bike competition by youthful tweed wearers. Glasgow's luxurious Blythewood Hotel aligns itself with Scottish heritage for tourists and other visitors by draping incorporating the iconic island tweed in fabric from furniture to lampshade coverings. However, downward revaluations in the Japanese yen currency create a potential problem by raising import prices. HTH and other tweed producers seek to cultivate new markets such as the formerly premier one in North America. Entrees include clothes carried by upscale stores such as Brooks Brothers, Saks Fifth Avenue, and Rag & Bone. For all such outlets a key appeal features Harris Tweed's attention to "details and heritage", along with the trendy sustainability of a nearly indestructible cloth. The December 2015 grant from Highland and Island Enterprises recognized HTH's success on the global stage. Multiplier effects emanate from the tweed industry generating associated funds from tourism, food-drink-boarding facilities, and creative endeavors such as handicrafts and performance events.

Weavers

The three most important of the several parts comprising the Harris Tweed industry are the independent weavers who choose what projects they want to work on, the Harris Tweed Authority whose mission is to maintain the integrity of the Orb mark and what it represents, and the private mills whose function lies with producing, supervising, and marketing the product and its parts. In the 1970s and '80s the weavers maintained a compulsory union through which the mills contracted for weaving work. Following the economic downturn and with the rise in demand for tweed over the last decade, some weavers entered into a voluntary association. This loose organization of weavers negotiated with the mills for a rise in the price paid for piecework and managed occasional disputes. While successful in recent interactions with the mills, the Weavers Association can persuade but not compel. The organization seems weak compared to its predecessor's position in the past and the reticence of some workers to formally join. A "free rider" problem remains with all weavers sharing the benefits accrued due to the increase in demand for tweed, but not all contributing to the organizational time and effort invested in a shared cause. Weavers are paid the same rate regardless of the mill, the complexity of the pattern, or weight of the material (traditional or lighter). Some keep both the single width Hattersley and the newer double-width Bonas Griffith loom to handle orders involving both.

By mid-2015 mill machines (Figure 7.3) turned out ten million pounds (500,000 meters) of product, employing 80 largely local workers. One hundred and forty off-site home weavers received mill-washed, carded, dyed and spun yarn on beams and bobbins for their looms, augmenting the on-site mill workforce. Vans visit weaver's homes to collect the woven unwashed cloth, taking it back to the mill to be finished, inspected and stamped with the Orb. Independent workers can purchase rolls of authenticated tweed to make their creations, marked with the HTA certification, if more than half of the total material is orb-approved wool.

Figure 7.3 Modern Harris Tweed Hebrides machinery

The training program at Lews Castle College, adjacent to the historic castle now serving as a museum, basically turns out mill workers. Weavers must seek training elsewhere such as requesting a practicing weaver to serve as a mentor. A generation or two ago the community council in Harris paid for an itinerant teacher to travel around villages, spending a month in each to teach students various weaving and mill-related skills in exchange for a small fee. The cost of a modern Bonas-Griffiths loom can be 20,000 British pounds – a substantial and discouraging sum for a young worker. Part of the proceeds from the electricity generated by the Shawbost windmill goes toward purchasing a loom that the Shawbost tweed mill then leases to would-be weavers. The mill there also maintains some spare parts for looms needing repairs. The increase in demand for cloth could support more young weavers, but industry structures designed to support a flagging business declined when times improved. The Shawbost mill is an exception to the reluctance of Lewis residents to support a plan for installing a large number of windmills to generate electricity by using brisk Barvas moor winds. Although bleak in some eyes, the moor was seen in the light of publicly expressed opinion as a traditional landscape that should be left undisturbed by voracious bird-eating modern machinery.

Retail Outlets

As textile producers the mill makes cloth, but does not control the uses to which the cloth is put following its sale. Mills sell surplus rolls of HTA-stamped tweed for a creative variety of products which must include at least 50% Harris Tweed in order to feature the Orb mark. Products are made and marketed by individual craft people and/or at retail outlets around the world. A small group of middlemen interface with the mills and retail sellers such as department stores. Designer retail outlets in the Hebrides featuring tweed products sell to locals as well as tourists seeking a unique souvenir.

In addition to "brick" storefronts around the island, "click" online websites feature Harris Tweed affiliated products from teddy bears to brooches, purses, scarves, hats, outerwear, and designer dresses, jackets, skirts and all types of clothing items. Anything made with cloth can become a tweed item, priced and promoted accordingly by affiliation with the name brand wool. Storeowners attend conventions, craft fairs, national and international department store exhibits featuring their affiliation with things British/Scottish. Japanese attendees reportedly swarm sites offering an English tearoom setting complete with scones, providing a cultural context for woolen wear and wares. The combination of food and drink creates an atmosphere that attracts and holds customers, whether whiskey, tea and scones or coffee and books, with product and setting matched to consumables to attract a market. A challenge for this part of the industry lies with government arrangements that investigate and make improvement suggestions for businesses but do not provide business loans or permit bank overdrafts for business expansion. This compares unfavorably to the U.S. where politicians and political entities frequently promote and support "business friendly" measures.

The future for Harris Tweed presently appears auspicious, but ambiguous fortune cookies can foretell a variety of outcomes that may turn out in murky ways. Unforeseen factors can lead to roller coaster rides such as those afflicting this product in the past. The geographic origins of global textiles are traceable by a glance at the tags in your own clothes closet, identifying items from east, south and southeast Asia to the Americas and beyond. The final chapter brings this discussion of a proxy for modernization processes to a contemporary summary conclusion. The mix of ubiquitous technology with distinctive core cultural identity features continues to pose daunting challenges to the survival of a way of life and fabric impossible to reproduce or duplicate in any other way. More than material is at stake in the struggles of a small Scottish island on the chilly, challenging edge of the North Atlantic.

CHAPTER 8

Future Patterns: A New Textile Trail?

"It is essential to continuing success that our industry should be exposed to new ideas, modern technology and an awareness of what is happening elsewhere in the textiles world . . . To the rest of the world, Harris Tweed may come from an island on the periphery but as seen from here, it is at the center of the universe!"
Brian Wilson, Chairman of Harris Tweed Hebrides, Shawbost

"Cultural traditions, cultural identity and cultural aspirations influence how we create and give meaning to our environment . . . and consolidate identities." Robertson 2009

Modernization's mix of technology enables industrialized mass production efficiencies. Preserving core elements of cultural identity requires combining efficient technologies with selected traditional elements and practices. Results play out with infinite variations in different geographic locations. The twists and turns of Harris Tweed's story show what may happen with attempts to carry on important elements and occupations from the past. The present requires new skills, stratagems and adaptability to global demands and markets, making profits while preserving the product's soul.

Proposals for continuing resuscitation of the Harris Tweed industry include the following:

1) New technologies are needed to replace or update machines. This is particularly required to improve production time to meet market demand;

2)   Training more weavers in addition to mill
          workers. This is the critical piece of the production
          chain that gives Harris Tweed its quality, historic
          appeal and price justification;

3)   Expansion into more Asian and other markets.
          Recapturing North American and Western
          European buyers is a key strategy. Research seeks
          the color and design preferences of each distinct
          market segment and location. Diversified markets
          may include upscale in Asia, upper middle in
          North America, and trendy 20-40 year old buyers
          in both.

Some similarities exist among the historical development situations in Lewis, China and Japan. Where a strong pro-growth interventionist central government existed, manufacturing developed. This was the case under the communist regime in China, which took power a century later than Japan's imperial industrialization launch as part of its push to modernize to survive the Western intrusions taking place in its large neighbor. Japan's pre-World War I model included a coterie of clannish crony capitalists. The Mitsui and Mitsubishi family firms, two outstanding examples, transformed medieval land-based wealth into new investments in industry. Textile conglomerate Ruyi represents modern China's mix of state-owned and quasi-private corporations. India and Lewis operated under a more colonial system with British overlords. Economic leadership came from capitalist occupiers and their military enforcers. In India this framework took the form of the British East India Company. The British home government left the Isle of Lewis in less-than-benign neglect. Control rested with the will of their capitalist titan owners. They proved largely unsuccessful in transferring their skill acquiring capital to improving their land's accompanying tenants. Lewis remained caught in its resolutely traditional ways, with a conservative culture common to its Asian counterparts. Lack of a central government with compulsion and capital to invest in local industrial conversion proved a critical impediment to progress through change.

Asia's importance as a market for Harris Tweed is clear, particularly seen in the presence of Japan. This island nation consumes upwards of ninety percent of all the Harris Tweed produced at present. Ties cultivated by Shawbost's Harris Tweed Hebrides (HTH) mill resuscitated the tweed textile as a viable Isle industry. Global ties form the basis of market expansion plans to other parts of the world. Recapturing the North American market, a major destination that nose-dived in the 1970s and has yet to get off the floor, remains a key target. Western Europe already parades Harris Tweed upscale fashions on its major couture runways.

The ability of HTH to cater to the fashion tastes of Japan pushed production in new, more modern directions. Colors created for a young market pop. Bright oranges, pinks, and bold light blues match Japanese tastes. Such flexibility showcases designers' abilities to fulfill requests. One notable search for a "sea color" led to a tonal combination with more aquamarine and less cobalt than traditional tweed blends. Openness to new color combinations cater to a younger demographic. An infinite variety of color mixes from the traditional palette characterize each strand of tweed. Discovery of thousands of traditional patterns placed in a storage warehouse by Haggas' Stornoway mill complement new visions. While the Kenneth Mackenzie mill restricted pattern variation, local independent weavers exercise their creativity to conjure new outlets and designs. The quality of Harris Tweed production meets even Japanese high standards. These carried Toyota to become a global car company giant, and advisor to other industries on production techniques known as lean manufacturing more sensitive to individual producers and efficiencies of time and energy. A commitment to flawless output and great attention to detail in both process and product outcome remain a distinguishing constant factor. Marketing innovations at Carloway and Shawbost mills promise to be a vital and vibrant part of Tweed's resuscitation.

The link to opening this huge market came through the connections of a particular team of individuals. Their worlds of politics and fashion combined to revive Harris Tweed Hebrides. HTH Creative Director Mark Hogarth contemplated a career as a geography teacher. He majored in political science at college and graduated to modeling in London. There he met then-Member of Parliament Brian Wilson at a fashion show in the year 2000 – while modeling a Harris Tweed outfit. Wilson hired Hogarth as a researcher, and became Minister of Trade in Prime Minister Tony Blair's Cabinet. Hogarth next spent an auspicious six months modeling men's fashions in Japan. This experience provided an invaluable understanding of and connection to that critical market. Both men joined forces at the new Harris Tweed Hebrides and found a receptive market in that fashion-conscious Asian country.

Foreign investment trends in textiles between the UK and China ebbed and waned on both shores. China functions as both an investor and a buyer of Harris Tweed. It remains a major consumer of men's jackets produced by Stornoway's Kenneth Mackenzie mill. This enterprise, formerly known under the brand name of Harris Tweed Scotland, produces a bit less than a quarter of the industry's output. SJR has approximately one-quarter stock ownership of the Carloway Mill. This emerging Asian textile group is typical of China's outward foreign direct investment expansion.

Surpassing the amount of capital that foreign firms invest in China is one result of China's "new normal" related to its "go-out" foreign investment policy. By the end of 2017, according to a British export post in December 2018, the UK for the first time had a slightly negative net foreign direct investment balance for the first time since records were kept by the government office. Inward FDI rose from 2016-17, more than outward investment flowed from the UK. The relationship with China did not follow this pattern, with investments of 103.1 billion pounds outbound to the Asian giant, and 88.4 billion coming to the UK. Most investments in the UK were predictably in high value sectors such as information technology and financial services, rather than manufacturing.

The major distinction of Lewis' tweed production lies in the early and continuously reinforced role of home-based weavers. Different outcomes reflect widely varying decisions by owners of the three Harris Tweed mills. Two of the mills' administrators extensively upgraded their in-house production equipment as Chinese investors advised. Carloway takes pride in utilizing machinery from the turn of the twentieth century. Each of the mills also made different target market decisions. Stornoway turns out a highly restricted number of basic men's jackets. These sell primarily to the Chinese market. Shawbost/Siabost aims for a high fashion, trendy and currently Japanese and European clientele. Carloway furnishes a variety of standard designs to the same but less extensive market.

The peripheral location of the production sites on the isolated Isle of Lewis appears to have little effect on Harris Tweed sales. Representatives travel the world to attend shows and network with clients. Modern technology shrinks distances between face-to-face encounters. The uniqueness of the product, created by its historical setting and labor arrangement including mandated local home weaving, remains its strength and distinction. The entrepreneur's vision makes the difference, finding points of intersection with demand and what is needed to meet it. In the case of Carloway, the new team of owners includes a former mill manager. Matched with the deep pockets of an oil and gas tycoon, she purchased the firm for the token price of a single pound. Previous management considered the arrangement preferable to taking further funds from the Chinese investment firm. This might have meant surrendering decision making power to an outside global conglomerate less familiar or concerned with Scottish ways critical to production success, as learned to his chagrin too late for the likes of Lord Leverhulme.

If imitation is the sincerest form of flattery, verbiage applied to the 2015 debut of wool products fashioned from the competitor wool of Peruvian alpaca acknowledged Harris Tweed's global success. Publicity echoing attributes applied to Harris Tweed extols alpaca's "rich history", "luxury fiber for global brands", "beautiful luster and depth of color". Wool from a high altitude sheep native to the Andes comes in a "wide color range" and is an "echo of traditions of the people". Using "state of the art technology", it is "unlike some wools, no itchiness". Fabric strength that "does not diminish with time" occupies a "prestigious position in home and international markets". The U.S. company Woolmark similarly advertised its new lines of wool rooted in "turn-of-the-twentieth century nostalgia". "Highlands" is "inspired by two trends becoming more evident: the coming back of the jacket and tweed or tweed look fabrics [with] . . . colors of Highland's nature". The London "Street Market" line evokes "ports on the shore of the English Channel". The image plays on the Anglo affiliation with woolen tweed, in this case supplied by an alternative animal native to the South American highlands.

Yet Harris Tweed's competitive advantage remains the human factor: the skilled lone weaver at work on the home loom in his highland shed. The Orb's stamp of quality supplies the time-honed assurance of a specific historic provenance evoking a specific place-based heritage. As Shawbost's Brian Wilson confidently declared in early 2018:

> "A lot of breath is wasted on worrying about the identity which Scottish goods should be marketed under . . . Harris Tweed benefits from having multiple identities: Hebridean (good for provenance), Scottish (good for woolens), British (good for fashion). The one that trumps them all is quality, without which the others would not get us very far."

Summarizing Development

The history of Harris Tweed began as a typical textile tale. Material came from dyed, spun and woven threads made by men and women in their homes. Identification with the place of production is also common to the other examples in this story. Competitive features are the outcome of a local style, promoted by an influential individual who helped create a market based on unique qualities of the cloth. Growth of the market served as a marker of success. Availability of technology to produce more material faster created a crucial series of decisions. These characterize different societies' responses to the modernization transition.

The material now known as Harris Tweed grew out of a particular time as well as place. The island's economy was already troubled when James Matheson purchased the Isle of Lewis in 1844 with his fabulous profits from opium-related trade. The ongoing Clearances compounded failure of the kelp industry. Onset of the potato famine two years later coincided with Lady Dunmore's discovery of tweed as a practical fabric for fashionable pursuits. Promotion to her peers coincided with concern for suffering crofters. Matheson proposed encouraging emigration to relieve population and starvation pressures. The 1890s saw establishment of several organizations to relieve crofter's poverty. Weaving this distinctive material encouraged cottage production by men and women, worked in with other agricultural chores. The granting of Britain's first trademark to Harris Tweed localized production further. Three successive Acts of Parliament in 1909, 1933, and 1993 confirmed the geography of production and confined the weaving to home production.

Many factors favored the rise of China's manufacturing strength. Textiles played a leading role as the key industry for field-to-factory transition in 19th century Shanghai's French extraterritorial enclave. The Paramount Leader of a rejuvenated China at the turn of the 21st century encouraged major companies to invest abroad. An economically weakened Britain and vulnerable Carloway Mill attracted this type of foreign investment. All played a consequential part in Shandong Ruyi's acquisitions.

Operating within a structural and historical framework, individuals at each stage mattered to the outcome. Formal recognition of the orb trademark symbol as an official coat of arms and a record sales year for Harris Tweed came in 2016. More good news involved the sale of the firm renamed "The Carloway Mill Ltd". The latest chapter in preservation began with the February 2017 announcement of Carloway Mill's sale. Former mill production manager Annie MacDonald and oil baron Anthony Loftus teamed up to buy the property for the munificent sum of one pound. This followed a tense year languishing on sale. Offshore investors participated as potential bidders. Previous owners sought to turn the mill over to an entity that understood and appreciated local ways of working. Profit generation was of secondary concern. A stripped down workforce continues on the renovated premises. Hope endures for a long-term revival.

Key questions in this examination of Harris Tweed's history as a modernization proxy concern what elements of past practices to retain as meaningful cultural identifiers. What new steps to adopt or adapt in pursuit of useful efficiencies of time and increased profit? Initial decisions frequently met with challenges requiring reaffirmation or modification. Concern lay with maintaining culturally as well as economically significant features. Demand also reflects a shifting market including fashion preferences of various ages, genders, income, cultural affinity. Appropriate workforce and production elements need training and upkeep through alternative occupations and machine technology.

Textiles serve as a proxy for processes beyond their physical utility. For Harris Tweed a major selling point is the element of place. Colors of flora and fauna evoke a distinctive history of struggled-over landscape. The Isle of Lewis and Harris speak the distinctive Scots Gaelic dialect, representing a daily life bond among its residents now reinforced in island schools. Economic arrangements such as crofting continue. The Free Church continues to exert a strong influence on the island of its birth. Traditionally distinctive dress such as kilts, tartans, and long scarves incorporate tweed. The wool fabric and the intertwined fates of the people and animals that produced it lend a heightened awareness of a tangled symbolic relationship. They feed and endanger each other in compliance with and resistance to powers above them both. Yet it is important not to overinflate the significance of a single product. Harris Tweed comes only from the Outer Hebrides, but the islands would keep their culture should both peat and tweed pass into time.

Colorful Past, Global Future

The story presented by an iconic textile features a global modernization rollercoaster ride from the mid-19th to the early 21st century. The firms producing Harris Tweed represent the cart. The double rail of converging tracks traces developments in Asia and the Outer Hebrides. Although major actions took place on the periphery of the world stage, transferable lessons learned exist, including the following:

- Ascending the modernization path is usually slow and difficult, but the downward dive is rapid and cyclical;
- A small number of key visionary individuals is frequently of outsize importance;
- A necessary step lies with choosing a core product feature (e.g., home weavers) with cultural resonance. Next step: adding technology to modernize the rest of the process;
- Companies need to stay attuned to the market and poised to pivot as conditions change. Historic examples include moves from North America to Japan and China - and potentially back again;
- Look for new applications to keep the product relevant and responsive to a main demographic. Examples include suit jackets, dolls, furniture covers, shoes and purses. Shawbost mill currently markets a range of outputs (Figure 8.1).

Preserving the place-ness of a product provides critical context. The selling of this image as a market ploy can fudge the reality in ironic ways. Several poster pictures advertise the Outer Hebrides as the ideal source for Harris Tweed. In one image a row of white sheep parades along a hillside path perched beside a blue *loch* (lake) under a lowering gray sky. One problem is that the sheep depicted are the local blackface rather than the cheviot breed used for the highest quality, softer wool tweed. They much prefer the flatter inland moor to the rocky hillside. Another rustic image pictures the production activity of a weaver working his loom inside a rocky, basket-strewn room. While the weaver is real, the loom is the seldom-used single width Hattersley. The setting is a museum-like restored "blackhouse". This tourist attraction is far grander than the actual humble shed setting where most weavers do their work - including the workrooms of the individual portrayed.

Figure 8.1 New products for expanding global market

Real people continue to live and rely on the work of these looms, proudly pursuing and preserving part of a traditional lifeway. A surge in demand for tweed produced in the successful, expanding Shawbost mill provides a source of pride. It also supplies much-needed employment. The continuation of Harris Tweed as a product depends on global as well as local market and economic factors. These also reflect the outcome of decisions by managers. Harris Tweed has found a way to retain local roots while branching out to a world market. The Outer Hebrides' most famous product continues in a peripheral geography with a larger future, with lessons for aspirants around the world seeking to sustain selected traditions that can aid a more prosperous and promising future.

ACKNOWLEDGEMENTS

Gratitude goes to a number of people who assisted the research and completion of this work. All errors, of course, should be attributed to its author. Able archivist Seonaid McDonald allowed me to do research in the wonderful archives of historic Lews Castle, just prior to the full public opening of the brilliantly renovated Lews Castle Museum. My cousin in Barvas is always a hostess par excellence, introducing me to various locations and lending her car for mill trips. My uncle, to whom this volume is dedicated, long ago demonstrated his prowess at both the weaving loom and bagpipes. And thanks to an aunt who, upon learning that my professorial interests lay in China's development, planted the initial seed of curiosity by confessing that "there is a black sheep in our family . . ." referring to the shared but ultimately unrelated name of Matheson, the opium trader.

Tour guides and former owners at Carloway Mill permitted me to interview them, during a visit by their Chinese investors. A number of Harris Tweed Hebrides workers also provided a tour, research material, and several interviews. Workers and former employees at Stornoway's mill joined the practitioners' chorus. Retail outlets handling Harris Tweed were generous with their time and information from their perspective. Several weavers gracefully permitted me to watch them work, demonstrating their craft in its setting on several machines. Interesting museums on Lewis showed historic weaving implements and products. The Stornoway public library and its helpful research assistants provided a collection of historic print materials such as newspapers noting significant events.

A friend and neighbor experienced in book publishing – and like me a "recovering academic" - guided me through the production process leading to my publisher and graphic designer. And of course, thanks to my patient assistant in all things, my husband Andy.

BIBIOGRAPHY

Anderson, Fiona. 2006. This sporting cloth: Tweed, gender and fashion 1860-1900. *Textile History* 37 (2): 166-186.

Bishop, Elizabeth. 2015. *Women's Work: The First 20,000 Years*. New York: W.W. Norton &Company.

Blake, Robert. 1999. *Jardine Matheson: Traders of the FarEast*. London: Weidenfeld & Nicolson.

Blanchard, Jean-Marc. 2011. Chinese MNCs as China's New Long March: A Review and Critique of the Western Literature. *Journal of Chinese Political Science* 16:91-108. DOI 10.1007/s11366-010-9131-1.

Cantin, Etienne. 2009. Modes of production, rules for reproduction and gender: the fabrication of China's textile manufacturing workforce since the late Empire. *Third World Quarterly* 30 (3): 453-468.

China Shandong Ruyi Group. 2016. http://www.chinaruyi.com/indexe.asp

Comhairle nan Eilean Siar. 2015. Factfile – Population. http://www.cne-siar.gov.uk/factfile/population/

Cort, Louise Allison. 1989. The Changing Fortunes of Three Archaic Japanese Textiles. In Weiner, Annette B. and Jane Schneider, eds. *Cloth and Human Experience*. Washington: Smithsonian Institution Press, 377 - 415.

Cox, Mabel. 1900. The Home Arts and Industries Association. *The Artist: An Illustrated Monthly Record of Arts, Crafts and Industries (American Edition)* 28 (247): 145-150. DOI: 10.2307/25581556.

Deacon, E.H. Jan. 14, 2014. Woven wonder: Harris Tweed is breaking new fashion frontiers. *European CEO*.

Dicken, Peter. 2007. *Global Shift: Mapping the Changing Contours of the World Economy*. New York: The Guilford Press.

Economic News Bureau. 2014. Reliance Industries Ltd to enter textile JV with China's Shandong Ruyi. 10 December. http://indianexpress.com/article business/business-others/reliance-industries-forms-textiles-jv-with-chinas-shandong-ruyi/

Economist. March 16, 2013. Harris Tweed loom and bust: An old industry goes back to basics. *The Economist*

Ennew, Judith. 1982. Harris Tweed: construction, retention and representation of a cottage industry. In Esther N. Goody, ed., *From Craft to Industry: The Ethnography of Proto-industrial Cloth Production*. Cambridge: Cambridge University Press.

Ernst and Young. May 27, 2015. Scotland secures 3rd best year on record for Foreign Direct Investment with Best Ever Performance from U.S. http://www.ey.com/UK/en/Newsroom/News-releases/15-05-27---Scotland-secures-3rd-best-year-on-record-for-Foreign-Direct-Investment-with-best-ever-performance-from-US.

Faison, Elyssa. 2007. *Managing Women: Disciplining Labor in Modern Japan*. Berkeley: University of California Press.

Geddes, Arthur. 1955. *The Isle of Lewis and Harris: A Study in British Community*. Edinburgh: Edinburgh U. Press.

Grace, Richard. 2014. *Opium and Empire: The Lives and Careers of William Jardine and James Matheson*. Montreal: McGill-Queens U. Press.

Hanemann, Thilo and Mikko Huotari . 2015. Chinese FDI in Europe and Germany: Preparing for a New Era of Chinese Capital. A Report by the Mercator Institute for China Studies and Rhodium Group. http://rhg.com/wp-content/uploads/2015/06/ChineseFDI_Europe

Harper, Catherine and Kirsty McDougall. 2012. The very recent fall and rise of Harris Tweed. *Textile* 10 (1): 78-99.

Harris Tweed Association. 2014. Information Pack. Stornoway: Harris Tweed Association.

Harris Tweed Hebrides/ Heriot-Watt University. 2015. *Creative Futures: The Heritage of Making for a 21st Century Textile Industry*. Glasgow Graphical House.

Hebrides News. 2013. Chinese Breakthrough for Harris Tweed. *Hebrides News* [http://www.hebrides news. com/harris_tweed_china%20_breakthrough_11313.html

Hunter, J. 2014. Reviving the Kansai cotton industry: engineering expertise and knowledge sharing in the early Meiji period. *Japan Forum* 26 (1): 65–87, http://dx.doi.org/10.1080/09555803.013.828767

Hunter, Janet. 2001. *The Islanders and the Orb: The History of the Harris Tweed Industry, 1835-1995*. Scotland: Acair Ltd.

Hutchinson, Roger. 2005. *The Soap Man: Lewis, Harris and Lord Leverhulme*. Edinburgh: Birlinn.

Ingles, Forbes. 2013. How tweed was my island. *British Heritage* 34 (5): 52-57.

Itochu. 2014. Itochu's Investment. https://www.itochu.co.jp/en/files/ar2012e_06.pdf

Jenkins, D.T. and K.G. Ponting. 1982. *The British Wool Textile Industry 1770-1914*. London: Heinemann Educational Books Ltd.

Keswick, Maggie, ed. 1982. *The Thistle and the Jade: A Celebration of 150 Years of Jardine, Matheson & Co.* Hong Kong: Mandarin Publishers Limited.

Lawson, Bill. 2008. *Lewis: The West Coast in History and Legend*. Edinburgh: Birlinn.

Le Corre, Philippe and Alain Sepulchre. June 2016. China abroad: The long march to Europe. Brookings Institute.

Le Pichon, Alain, ed. 2006. *China Trade and Empire: Jardine, Matheson & Co. and the Origins of British Rule in Hong Kong, 1827-1843.* Oxford: Oxford University Press.

Liang Xiaohui, Liu Xin, Ren Xiaolei, and Zheng Jian. 2013. The Regional Transition of China's Manufacturing Industries and its Impact on Social Responsibility. www.swedenabroad.com

Maclean, Murdo. 6 February 2015. Teachers to ditch English and
    use Gaelic only in six Western Isles schools. The Press and
    Journal.   https://www.pressandjournal.co.uk/
    fp/news/islands/western-isles/483239/gaelic-to-be-main-
    language-at-six-western-isles-schools/
Macleod, Angus. History of Harris Tweed. *The Angus
    Macleod Archives.* www.angusmacleodarchive. org.uk/.
Macgregor, Alasdair Alpin. 1948. *Behold the Hebrides!
    Wayfaring in the Western Isles.* London:
    W. & R. Chambers, Limited.
Mackenzie, W.C. 1903. *History of the Outer Hebrides.*
        London: Love & Malcomson Limited.
Magnusson, Magnus. 2000. *Scotland: The Story of a Nation.* New
        York: Grove Press.
Marsh, E. 2008. Fabric of the Community. http://wwd.com/globe
    news/fashion/fabric-of-the-community-1885307/].
Mathias, Peter. 1969. *The Industrial Nation:1700-1914.*
        London: Methuen.
Merriman, John.1996. *A History of Modern Europe from the
        Renaissance to the Present.* New York: W.W. Norton.
Moss, V. 2015. Harris Tweed: The Wool to Succeed.
        The Telegraph, 25 April.
[http://www.telegraph.co.uk/luxury/womens-style/69209/harris-
tweed-the-wool-to-succeed.html]
Mould, D., D. C. Pochin. 1953. *West-Over-Sea: An Account of Life
        in the Outer Hebrides set against the legendary and
        Historical Background.* Edinburgh: Oliver and Boyd.
Murphy, Joseph. 2013. Place and exile: resource conflicts and
        sustainability in Gaelic Ireland and Scotland. *Local
        Environment* 18 (7): 801-816.
Myers, Diana and Susan Bean, eds. 1994. *From the Land of the
        Thunder Dragon: Textile Arts of Bhutan.* London: Serindia.
Nakamura, Naofumi. 2015. Reconsidering the Japanese industrial
        revolution: Local entrepreneurs in the cotton textile
        industry during the Meiji era. *Social Science Japan
        Journal.* 18(1): 23-44.

National Records of Scotland. 2015. Scotland's Census 2011:
   Inhabited Islands Report.
   http://www.scotlandscensus.gov.uk/
   documents/analytical_reports/Inhabited_islands_report.pdf.
New York Times. February 14, 2016. China's Wealthy Move
   Money Out as Country's Economy Weakens. 1,10.
Platman, Lara. 2014. *Harris Tweed: From Land to Street.* London:
   Frances Lincoln Ltd.
Pomeranz, Kenneth and Steven Topik. 2006. *The World that Trade
   Created: Society, Culture, and the World Economy 1400 to
   the Present.* Second Edition. Armonk, NY: M.E. Sharpe.
Robertson, Mairi. 2009. Aite Dachaidh: Re-connecting people with
   place – island landscapes and intangible heritage.
   International Journal of Heritage Studies 15 (153-162):
   DOI: 10.1080/13527250902890639
Ronayne, Megan. 2015. Manufacturing textile futures: Innovation,
   adaptation and the UK textiles industry. In Bryson, John,
   Jennifer Clark, and Vida Vanchan, eds., *Handbook of
   Manufacturing Industries in the World Economy,*
   Cheltenham, UK: Edward Elgar Publishing.
Sinclair, Marion, ed. 1996. *Hebridean Odyssey: Songs, Poems,
   Prose and Images.* Edinburgh: Polygon.
Spybey, Kat. February 16, 2016. Into the dragon's den
   of Chinese retail.http://www.drapersonline.com/
   7004692.article?WT.tsrc...Accessed 2/16/16.
Thompson, Francis. 1984. *Crofting Years.* Edinburgh: Luath Press
   Ltd.
Tidball, Harriet. 1961. *Woolens and Tweeds. Shuttle Craft
   Monograph Four.* Coupeville, WA: ShuttleCraft
   Books, Inc.
United Nations Conference on Trade and Development.
   https://unctad.org/en/pages/PublicationWebflyer.
   aspx?publicationid=2297
UNCTAD. 2018. World Investment Report: Investment
   and New Industrial Policies. https://unctad.org/
   en/PublicationsLibrary/wir2018_en.pdf

Walcott, Susan. 2011. "One of a Kind: Bhutan and the Modernity
    Challenge" *National Identities* 13: 253-266.
Walcott, Susan. 2014. *A Profile of the Furniture Manufacturing
    Industry: Global Restructuring*. Business Expert Press.
Walcott, Susan. 2014.Capitalist China Comes to the Southeastern
    United States: Localizing Foreign Direct Investment in the
    Carolinas and Georgia. *Southeastern Geographer* 54 (3):
    291-307. Chapel Hill, NC: U. of North Carolina Press.
Walcott, Susan. 2018. "Chinese National Identity and Social
    Networks" in D. Kaplan and G. Herb, eds., *Scaling
    Identities: Nationalism and Territoriality*. Lanham,
    Rowman & Littlefield, 203-220.
Weiner, Annette B. and Jane Schneider, eds. 1989. *Cloth and
    Human Experience*. Washington: Smithsonian Institution
    Press.
Wylie, Gus. 2003. *Hebridean Light*. Edinburgh: Birlinn.
Zemin, Jiang. 2002. "Build a Well-off Society in an All-Round
    Way and Create a New Situation in Building Socialism with
    Chinese Characteristics". Report delivered at the 16th
    National Congress of the Communist Party of China
    http://en.people.cn/200211/18/eng20021118_106984.shtml

INDEX

CPSIA information can be obtained
at www.ICGtesting.com
Printed in the USA
FSHW020853110120
65988FS